Schizo in Love

Jeannie Choi

Fulton Books, Inc.
Meadville, PA

Published by Fulton Books 2021

ISBN 978-1-63860-925-4 (paperback)
ISBN 978-1-63860-926-1 (digital)

Printed in the United States of America

Introduction

Only upon a whim or conceived idea could a world be created, and from that commission, this person formed and was molded. Do I have the capacity as an individual? I have such to merit or demerit it logical, don't I? I may say this in a general tone, but note, this thought has no need of persisting allowance. Even so, having your ear, I have no permission to carry my existence into mandatory involvement whatsoever. If I willingly do so, I may believe it a struggle. I have seen myself do my best to please people in a way that in all expectations had no immediate reward, except the company of complacent manners. Did it produce much of an effect on how I compliment others or give a friendly exchange? Probably not. I must resound with my singlehood though as to being pretentious for the benefit, so I came in tune with my talent to be articulate.

When I had become involved with my boyfriend, I noticed, in gradation, my will to please had dissipated. It was almost difficult, at certain times, to render the memory of the success. I assumed that it was excessively in high spirits to be catered to and unnecessary that I must see my end. When I understood that other goals were needed to be done, the emotional, painstaking energy had to be reinvented to those things. No matter how meticulous, it is now forgotten to drainage. The frivolity has turned into an urgency to do the importance required, in spite of having a boyfriend. I don't have to accommodate the idea of another half but the reality of action and duty. In actuality, more simple and real than what I've believed formed.

It's not that I'm not satisfied with life. I am rather tolerating my self-contemplation. Who am I as an Asian American? Yes, it's true, but more so, I go without reminding myself that I am a schizophrenic. This is the capacity of my ability to maintain my identity—

to refute the truth. Can I relearn "What am I going to do now?" after being diagnosed at age fourteen to be mentally ill. It was really difficult to boil it down to commitment terms to what my label was because I was experiencing these hallucinations. Though not going to lie, I wanted a different life, a happy life. Ever since then, there was an array of modes and this evolution I had to succumb to. Some thoughts were taking hold to challenge. There were voices from forceful realms, sounding audible and putting me in a ruminating-looking state. From an outsider's view, I would be silent. The only positivity of a teenager diagnosis is that I can get used to the initial sufferings by myself. But that hasn't stopped me from delving into an active psychotic breakdown, where I am visibly distraught and extreme in public.

This started in my midtwenties. I thank God for my parents being my caretakers, of course, when I lived at home while attending high school and part of college. Being that young, things were still new. Adults still had the ability to treat me like I had the best of the future at youth. What made me fine with an idea at a time of psychosis? To act out in an absolute conviction, then would be called sanity if left alone, right? A healthy mind can completely leave it alone with distraction. Getting to work and attending to hobbies are coping skills. A psychotic breakdown is defined, in my words, as a stability falling apart with no explanation and no remedy until it passes through. The only reason I had not been taking my medicine for months on end. Yet when the fogginess arrives and behavior goes away, It can't be stopped, and I'm not able to ask for help correctly. I can't shake off or realize I'm caught up in this schizophrenic psychotic breakdown.

This flow, in other words, is because I have given over to the delusion—a false belief, also disguised as a command, to act on. In otherworldly times, when having a chance to move is in a matter of minutes, I'd feel paralyzed; knowing I'm not in a stable time in life somehow. My racing heart tells me I'm an idiot, so my next move better be the right opportunity to get going or else, even though it's not the direction, I need to go. Nonsensical fear gets me to respond to these psychotic delusions. When it is shameful it throws any self-worth out the window. I don't think it through. Instead, my illness makes me pinpoint the single idea and hold it to fruition. No way would I be able to let that go until this belief I grasped would go nowhere.

Chapter

My Backstory

I had put comedy first over God. A contradiction to the life I wanted to pursue led me to be on the streets, homeless in Hawaii. All I wanted was to get ahead in the business of performing for my peers or for everybody. Hey, maybe it would affect my career when or if it ever takes off.

It wasn't just the stressors of open mic comedy night. As it was the need to get to my full-time job, make it on time there, and then get up on stage at the 10:00 p.m. showtime with the 8:00 p.m. sign-ups. All this before the start of graveyard shift at midnight. My first night debuting for comedy had been spring. In the summer, I would have had to move out of an old place, quit one job, get another, then by the end of summer, I had no jobs, no place to stay. Then I remembered my appointment with hosting an open mic, so I rushed with determination to get my comedy mind together or any sort of function, but use of notes worked. Although I mostly cracked up and laughed for no reason at my own jokes.

Prior to moving into a new place in Honolulu, the old place had been closer to the open mic venue. It was a great location. I decided to switch to save money. And the fact that the room was behind a garage, the entry was the door into the garage and no kitchen, just a bathroom. It was less than a studio. All I had was a microwave and bathroom amenities, but I had a bed and drawer/closet. It made the new place to live in less of a downgrade, yet it looked like a rub and tug massage parlor with a kitchen and four rooms, with the shower room having a massage table. This was the last place I lived in as a single lady, even though I had a male roommate for the first time in my life. Strictly platonic, we hung out a few times since the weather is nice every day in Hawaii. I worked off my rent by working for the landlord at the dessert eatery they owned, about a block away. It was at this same time that I worked here as a cashier, and I was a cashier at a drug store overnight. Three jobs technically, and on top of that, I participated in open mics for comedy, poetry slams, and improv shows.

The thrill of being able to come up with jokes had me set out to use as much of this creativity, but one night, it took a toll as I sat in the kitchen and decided on this wonderful, outrageous joke. It made me laugh out loud while alone, a little too loud that my temporary roommates, who were there for air bed and breakfast board (the landlord rented out the other rooms for profit), got pretty annoyed. Of course, I came in contact with them the next day, but by then, I became completely nuts. I sensed I didn't know what to do with my frustration because I felt motionless with the heaviness and paranoia stemming toward an uncanny anxiety. I acted out like I had the right to be upset for them to be residing there. Next thing that happened was the landlord said that I needed to leave. He said that I'm no longer allowed to live there. I had no permission to return, but I snuck in some days while I was on the street to either pick up my food stamp card or wash my garments or transfer my luggage. I told my male roommate to hold on to it, only to have it gone or taken from me like it wasn't even mine. There were some nice dresses in that big, red, Izod suitcase.

Truth was, I wanted to live in with a prostitution ring leader, I suppose. I believed we were moving along, and I knew the hotel we had been at most times than other hotels, as well as the manager. He even tried setting me up with other guys. Months later after being off the street, I attempted to retrieve my suitcase, only to find it missing or otherwise; and the call to the manager ended up in an argument saying I married the "leader," who I claimed should've been responsible. More than once I had been convinced of a chance of companionship, or in my case, more of a delusion for hopes that I have a place to sleep with a good night's rest.

The other dragging conviction of the delusion was thinking I had meant to be taken advantage of. These clients, who appeared or what not loomed psychotically as a mindless snag to fulfill a "life" I never knew of, made it hard to let go of that pull. Instead of making the escape so easy where I could ask or run for help after damaging the balls out, I never did. Funny thing is, I had not been trapped. I did these guys on my own free will. It was not by coincidence I'd get a booty call, and I'd go to the hotel in broad daylight. This number would be the number I would memorize and treat like my best companion, yet he could have at least fed me well. Instead, Scott used my body. Scott also used another person to pose as Scott and have him pick me up by a random stranger, parked his car by me, and there goes the beginning of what would be my trafficked life. As I said yes to getting into his car, he told me, "I'm not the one, but I'll lead you to the one."

I'll remember him as the gummy penis, recorded in a minivan, and how I had attempted yelling in another language. Prior to the minivan incident, within an hour, he has taken me to a grassy hill open for the resident houses nearby to see us procreating. I think it was a test. I honestly think he was set up, and his life was at stake to make a video. He is not the ring leader though. (I would like to say there were good Samaritans, but these "friends" hadn't asked what was going on in my days or nights. They just helped be with me for some of the nights platonically, yet I never got to really sleep). That very first night I had been "abducted," I ended up at a hotel, and to this day, I don't know the name of it. The hotel room had twin beds, where I lay stomach down the entire night. During which out of alertness, I felt hands massaging my shoulders. I looked back to see that there were males, and that the male masseuses traded off because I witnessed different pairs of shorts and heights.

The morning after, I wake up to find in the other twin bed a man about six feet tall, I guess, lying down sideways. Silently, he covered his eyes and brought them down to the point of his face closing his eyes, only to bring it up. I still hadn't gotten to really see what he looked like, as he repeated this gesture so that I would not recognize him. There was something about his genitals. My boyfriend has once mentioned a simile after that fact to "a rubber band around it?" This scene I was in was unfamiliar, for there was liquor in the bathroom, with a bowl filled to the rim, and a full bottle on the side of the sink. I needed to ruin this spectacle of what it seemed with me in here with him, and I poured the expensive bottle of liquor down the drain.

He soon came in after asking what am I doing. Notice, this was my first day trafficked with a stranger (yet nothing happened that day) and a supposed one-night stand, and it looked like I was concerned about his alcoholism. In a flux and whirlwind, I still hadn't got a good look at him; and just like that, the other Scott retrieved me from the room and took me to his white minivan. And we drove off to Leonard's bakery to get malasadas. He told me, "I'm so glad you are here."

Then off to the Ohia West. Now, I believe he had another Scott, a third Scott to look like him through plastic surgery. He's got it all planned out. I took a good guess, his name is Steve Cohen. On the way out of the Ohia West, the next morning, I stroll out with an older man if I remember. I'll call him Scott Behran, the one I lose my celibacy with. He told the clerk at the counter to check out of the hotel. Co-a-ten. Co-a-ten. At least four times. The guy behind says its Coates. Like he should know better, he's been using the room. My first experience copulating had been twelve years prior, and the guy wanted to add me on Facebook since then as J. H. Culleton. Coincidence? I never knew he had another last name.

After that fateful night and the next night with the gummy penis in the minivan, came the inception of taking steps to a level I could not get out of. After the malasada pastry run, I may have fallen for the guy that was the ring leader, that looked like the one on the first day. Well, we'll call him Steve, and Steve had been in my vicinity of making my body a meal that the lions share. I'm not one to market myself on the street, but like I said, I had Steve's number. And someone booty called or texted me with his number. More than one person had his number. I'm sure I was seen as a hooker, but it was Steve who knew where I was walking, and I got into his car. This had happened more than once. Probably knows my GPS through my phone number. Weird thing is, I never downloaded an app. Who does he work for?

At an incoherent state, there was no need to ask verbally or have any paper contract for me to comply into copulation. It's what he wanted, and I took on the role or the action to go for sexual behavior all in. How unreal it was. I didn't realize this was still a traumatic event. I told myself, "It's okay."

But honestly, I was so ashamed of losing my celibacy. I wanted a new life after it's all over, I prayed. At the moment, I had no way of saying no to what seemed to be an opportunity that arrived in a favor of vanity in the name of promiscuity. The vanity surely came in sheep's clothing. I craved the consistency of attention, though the stable me would have declined from the get-go, but now, the spout has opened. You know what they say. I'm still guilty, I had to be. I let the personality of street whore envelope me. I remember the wet, soaking, drenched feeling that by own will or force I was unable to clean or dry off. It was an impossibility to push away, what I say, this "friendliness, and trusting to a dangerous situation or the invite to a stranger's car." A break from the norm and a break from the regular harassment when celibate, that is.

There was one van that looked like a cocktail van used for parties. There had been a young driver, and he was cruising by slowly on the street. And I noticed him as he perhaps made himself noticeable at least a tad bit. I wanted to be off the street for at least that night and convinced "trusting" him would be worth it or at least guessing safe. Praying for a platonic night didn't come easy, and upon getting into the van, I just felt it. How the night or gathering would end and still I couldn't run. I didn't feel like I'd have somewhere to be that night in town on the street alone. I had a backpack on me, and with it, I picked up a trinket bong made of metal no bigger than a hand. After spending the night at the young man's place, I deliberately, or psychotically, left my backpack with my belongings there, thinking I'd never see them again, especially leaving the room he stayed in. And how we got into a van and seeing a man I hadn't seen in years that I met at the Potter's House church back in 2001. And he said,

"Your van is ready now," do I sensed and picked up meanings. Once the young man was hostage, as another porn recorder where 'life' at stake, and Zar was from Potter's House. The pastor at Potter's House, his name was, I guess, Timothy, maybe its Steve now or Scott. Don't accuse, right? The church closed down a year or two later, I'm guessing in 2001 or 2002. But what was Zar up to? I never saw him again after that. The young man was a sex slave, and how I know this was because of the STI. It was obvious, and I thought it could be worse for the men.

Well, for Steve and his naughtiness. He brought me to a hotel room already used and occupied with the Vaseline jar I bought and owned until he got a hold of it. Even someone's slippers were still there. I mean did we have a time slot or something? As for a piece of what I owned, remember the trinket bong no bigger than a hand? Well, it ended up in that hotel room as I looked around while Steve was sleeping. I took that trinket with me. It was covered in a familiar-colored substance. He slept after he weighed out his meth and smoked it and after we copulated.

I peered through an iPhone lying around. It wasn't active. There was only a picture selfie of Scott sleeping and a young girl with a tongue piercing. Seemed like a wild night. Which brings me to the time there was another hotel. And this was the hotel I felt safe leaving my clothes. I spent the day, and when trying to enter the Ebb Tide, there were two men guarding. I was sure, at least, I could get in I don't know why since there wasn't much communication obviously. It was very much the case when I barged in and that I walked up to the room that I believed was ours, me and Steve's, knocked, but it couldn't be heard because there were young teenage girls in there having a party. I believed they were teens. Loud and noisy. I was so mad. I stormed out of the patio/lobby, out the gate, and only to be smacked in the head. I punched him back. How dare he hit me. We went at it a few times, and I was on the ground. And a few other men, my peers I'll call them, asked him, "Why did you hit her three times?" I hit him three times too, then kicked him in the pants until I felt my foot was tased. After that, he pinned me down. What I got out of this was that he was assigned for my sake and my sake only.

I may have been on the street for a month or less, considering I've been in the hotel room or attempted by my friend to have me sleep in his car. But if it means not having my own bed, I've been homeless over a month. This one night, my endeavor to take a bus to the other side of the island failed, and I ended up near some youth at the skateboard park. The exception were JP and the man who offered me his cigarette. I veered off to take a drag. I heard the man laughing like he was drugged and then abruptly silent. Not a minute after, JP goes, "For the kids," a couple times.

The kids were unusually quiet. I don't know what happened to the man. I tried not to notice. I ended up going off and away out of town with JP. To make a long story short, he read my hormonal changes after a dip in the ocean. He had a tarp ready. I was already in a bikini, and before I knew it, he lie on top of me while I was on my stomach. And this was the first time I met the guy, not even three hours upon meeting. He looked into my backpack, took out shiitake mushrooms, and stole my tiny bag and sunglasses right in front of me. We have a second copulation with a youth in the hot tub of the hotel (this is outside). I told JP there's something wrong with what I saw, and JP took out a machete and started walking away. Good riddance.

Although, I met up with him again when I have made a boyfriend. How fleshly and lustful that was to compromise my Christianity, where no goal, no future mattered except to have this enjoyment of the "natural" yet so "glamorous" indecency. I had met a companion in Chinatown that had been a benefit and not a deficit, that I slept with part-time only because I couldn't sleep, and it was completely platonic. His name would be Pierre. He had been the angel who had helped me sleep at the cemetery, a small private one. He laid out his tarp, and it seemed he slept wistfully, except when one night it drizzled. I kept on being restless. It felt difficult to sleep so I roamed.

The next morning, we walked back downtown to Rivers of Life Missions facility, where they feed pastries and coffee. During the day, we would spend time at the library. He'd read books, and I'd look for books. But when I sat down to read, it was so tenuous like there really was no use. Parting from Pierre led me away from Chinatown into another town. I had my EBT card by then for snacks and meals. I had to walk to my old address, only to find my card came in the mail. The only important card I had now since my one trip to the beach led my belongings in a backpack stolen. Inside was my driver's license, passport, social security card, small business plan maybe, and my cell phone! The phone kept me close to ones I just met. Actually, a few men or a couple at a time, both good and bad. My stability felt close to gone when my phone was gone too. It would seem my life had come to this hopelessness, ongoing psychosis, and me being simply out of my mind and took drugs when offered.

To make it easier for me as a schizophrenic, I probably needed someone with me in my journey. It was difficult to feel like I had a future or a career. I felt confident when a day passed or a goal was fulfilled, but some days, it felt a bit cloudy and strenuous. To be happy, I needed to keep heading toward the bigger target. While on the streets, I couldn't figure out my past, my present being the hardest of times, or even think of the future. I wondered why I had to deal with this now, as in to have a relationship. Danny being the very help, unlike the others that didn't remain platonic because friendships were automatically friend-zoned. Daniel, I met one day back in town at a shopping mall with traffic-lined streets on both sides. He was on one side of the mall. I easily could've walked in the opposite direction of where he was at. What inclined me to go and stay and for what reason, I don't know. The seating rock wall was where he sat on the sidewalk. Someone who constantly strummed "Guantanamera" on his guitar had sat there for a consecutive of days beside him. He probably went home for the night though, of course.

Danny was a different sight altogether, and I stood by him and waited for him to start a conversation. He asked about how my abrasions got on my leg. I told him it's been a wild ride. He had a Band-Aid, and the rest was history. I followed him out of the mall for a day of walking. First to the beach, I believe, where I took a shower. It was enclosed, so it was more comfortable. He had soap on hand and a solution suitable for my abrasion. He was my new companion but not my last. I returned to JP for a moment, though it could've been marijuana. And that must've been my selfish move and what I took on quickly, I noticed, were also JP's motives. On a happy note, Danny said we met years ago. I just don't remember.

Seems quite peculiar with Danny, who I could trust, but it turned out, I unabashedly ditch him out of fear or anxiety. I was not convinced being alone would be better. It's just that I was preoccupied by either meeting up with Danny or going back to the Rivers of Life Missions facility. Thinking maybe there was something or someone there for me. My ride was becoming impatient.

"Take me away from Danny," I told her. Why? I do not know. I got off on the street where this time, no one was around. I got really scared that a creep would pop out around the corner, so I grab a beer bottle. I was still scared. And that's when a creep did show up, and it's JP. But instead of running away, I ran toward him. You see, this night there's more to the story. It had been Thanksgiving, and I got into a scuffle where I ended up with a cut on my head. JP knew somehow and brought me to a girl who offered me lotion and petroleum jelly and a pair of slippers. She looked like my friend, but something was eerie about the shade of coloring of her skin tone and aura or maybe it was the night. She looked at me and said, "Remember JAPE."

Finally, me and JP walked away to sleep soundly on the park grass. Just because this morning came unscathed by him didn't mean it's going to get better. I asked him if he was a Christian. No, he was Muslim. I continued to believe Muslim was partly a believer. Either way, this would not make me equally yoked. Being with JP meant a few nights on Merchant Street, not a very good place. It's where the homeless pitch up tent for the nights. I slept on cardboard. I knew the definition of survival sex, and JP seemed to make it like that. Meaning, put up or die. By this point, I didn't freak out from fear or acted like I needed to because for one it wasn't a familiar emotion at this point, and I was scoping out the horizons of what psychosis was leading me into next. I would never want to have sex with my friends as it seemed I had been taken advantage of by wicked men.

The next morning of the last of the few nights and days spent with JP, we were at the Rivers of Life Missions facility. And the awareness came to me of the landline available for use to anyone who wanted to make calls after breakfast. I was excited to remember Daniel's phone number and wholeheartedly tried not to screw it up or forget it as I repeated back in my head. Going back to JP physically not only made me feel bad but that I had smoked marijuana for the first time with him. Now that I heard Danny's voice over the phone, the exhilaration turned to nervousness as I thought of how I had to escape the grasp of JP that day to meet up with Danny. I told Danny to be at the library, yet when I hung up, it was still nerve-racking as my plans fell along with JP's. It didn't have to, I suppose, yet we ended up at Fort Street Mall. And I couldn't get up or budge to start walking to library. I wanted desperately to do so. But sure enough, lo and behold, Danny walked up and said, he thought I'd be at the library. So casual and pure, so full of love. I was stricken to break down, tell him what JP and I did, but I just told him he had to say bye to JP and let him know I'm leaving. JP went, "Will I see her again?"

I felt relieved to leave JP and the mall than to decipher what he meant by that. It's like the need to the simple things went unnoticed. Surviving at best, and for me, it was getting on with what was at hand or who I was with. I didn't even take into account what day it was or what month. Having Danny by my side, I felt happy and then, all in a heap that stuff happened while we were apart. I didn't want to be away from him again, yet in a heated argument, he left to walk away ahead of me to the place where we slept at night (at the college campus). Only I didn't follow him that night. A fateful night. I was alone, near the college campus and knowing my way around, I knew I had to sleep or lay down. I find a spot by the florist shop by 7-11. When not even an hour passed, three men stood in a huddle, hovering near by me. I watched them gather for two minutes.

One of them told me to follow him as he took his bike with him behind 7-11 to a small park. I had my backpack and a crossbody purse, but the backpack I rested on the fence as we arrived to the part of the secluded park. We smoke a cigarette. He took out a contorted wavy shaped meth pipe. He showed me a bag of pink ice meth, added it to the pipe, and took a hit, and I took a few hits as well. After this exchange, he ended up with my phone, and I'm on the ground. He told me because he did this for me, I got to do something for him. And he took off his pants enough where I see his flat, squidly penis. Once he hit my head and I put my lips to his thing but went no further. I started singing a gospel and pray. I wanted to get out of this predicament, and finally, I ran and left my backpack behind. My crossbody bag on me had a driver's license. The one thing I decided to take care immediately was to get a new one. I had $5 on me when my friend gave me the money to get a bus pass, yet I opted in getting a driver's license.

My ID picture looks all disheveled. It came to me in wonder, *Would I have run sooner if the guy didn't tell me the three people in the distance are Chinese girls out to get me?* He was lying. After I made my escape, the guy who nearly raped me, who had my phone and my backpack, started laughing while looking at my phone. I made my way near the exit of the park, and the three persons were males. And one of them asked me, "What did he do?"

And I was out of breath, only to mention with a little bit of communication that I am not a happy camper. The two started their way toward the area, and one stayed back. I was glad I could say they were on my side yet sad because I don't know what happened to him. Afterward, I ran to closest convenience store, 7-11, and asked to use phone to call 911. Police arrived to speak to me, and I spoke in such frantic tone and speed, and it figured with the meth. If I wasn't sure that I had meth in my system, I went to the psych ward that night and getting a urine test got it concluded.

I wondered if my newfound boyfriend had still been thinking of me when we were apart, and I really hoped he would visit me here at the psych ward. I wanted to call my boyfriend, and it happened. Danny visited me throughout my stay at the hospital. He cared. I got out of there a month later, and a shelter was my mode of residence. I was, apart from Danny, where I wanted to be closer. We hung out at the beach and that was all right, but three months after getting out of psych ward, we moved in together in a homeless transition shelter as a couple.

2
Chapter

A Little about Daniel

My boyfriend must have a diagnosis, he's got to. It's the detaching from a "programming" that he veers off. When in normal circumstances, it is possible to accomplish in hope. And with it, it takes understanding because his past determined his mode of action, like a definition of a younger kid with a personality trait. For me, I tried to make it an indifference to what he may, well, would've caused an uproar or otherwise in the community. In respect to his own life and hometown, these are my unhealthy observations spoken aloud.

If there is an unconscious shift between me and him, it was only known by what I feel. He couldn't take back or get from me what was of extreme importance. The attitude I have toward this explosion that has happened had me at fault, and I called it his "programming," to not be able to control his words toward effective, loving communication. Having every praise as it may come to him, he may be doing his best to get out a speech, and yet, it turned out the way it does. And it's funny the harshness of mental exhaustion or remorse on how damaging it was. The sending out of its effect in this tirade. This was why mental illness was unrelatable to those who never experienced it.

The unnerving effort of getting out of a situation that has placed me with him had got me reeling with, "This is a joke!" Or "I don't deserve this," or "this doesn't have to happen." But what if it does? Because this is a personality that I can't change and who I have to live with. I must love the person even if there are demons and even if the situations rise. In my case, I almost want to imagine someone mannerly, anybody else out of him, but its ultimately my choice to implicate the fact that he had loved. In certain times, it's what suffering lends out and am I able to judge correctly that silent cry and fight through to love instead? But never can he escape the diagnosis. When there's an urge, he cannot control to use an "alternative truth," and this, with the emotions he wants expressed or to prove himself, was acceptable.

I want to accept Daniel. I knew he was different. I was left, one way or another, in perplexity how he would do his part in the relationship being "different." Would he want something in return that can make him "feel" he is doing good? And that his way is being done? The one thing I ran into was a blockage that had me unsettled and pining for a true answer. The ultimatum to figure worth was, "What would have our relationship work out?" The virtue to love and be loved is considered in deciding the factor stemming from the other person looking like a selfish brat. If the solution presumably is to let go and to forgive my boyfriend of his carelessness, then fine. It's my consummation of why this is a hubbub in the first place come into play.

I remembered reading books on how women believe an ideal pursuit from a man is a fairy tale, sweep-me-off-my-feet type of story, where she gets rescued from the life of singlehood that oh so constrained her. I don't recall such a time where it is nearly that restricting. Now that my boyfriend has given me a definition of cohabitation. I believe females have access to the togetherness and knowledge prior to winning her mate. I almost can say life before Daniel has less incomparable suffering. Seeing as I have no one else to care about 24-7.

Moments had me fully aware I was no longer experiencing the freedom of singlehood. I mourned the fact and tried not to exasperate the idea of any form of better life that could be mine. I have been given what I have been given. Anybody else can tell me I can do better and resolve the issue by picking men who could truly love me. The remorse is energy dissolved; energy spent. I do my own thing by dismissing the opinions of me having everything well on everybody's mind. It's difficult. Imagining that good life or good will sounds really satisfying. But I'm not going to drop ship and jump out for a dream, when maybe this relationship could work out because it's the "disorder," and it can get better. Or at least his soul is in intact, and when that's all good, then things do get better.

I know well of other's opinions and that they mean well. When these questions arise, "Do you want to stay where you're at?" I can honestly read my soul and admit to myself, "It's not the same mistake. No, this is not going to be an experience to remember and with regret nonetheless."

Instead, I'm going to work this with him. No matter how hard it is with our lives, and especially, it'll be between us. Not always, but surely to the extent, we need help and we get help. This is the component of my character at this point. Can I handle that I have a frustrating time? Other than that, I am thinking back on my dumbfounded silence, if any, and how I must've coldheartedly refuted their two cents. But that isn't exactly the truth. I wasn't belligerent. I spoke maturely, like how I need to confirm. And I had the seriousness, and they took me serious as well.

I can understand where their care is originating from, whether there were evidential proofs leading to protectiveness, but I must state a paradox. Even strangers can provide a sort of strange stare, and with Daniel, I have sensed none. I stayed with my boyfriend because of the patience in me brought me this far. And along with that is his routine conviction to provide goodness and effort. It's not a constant fantasy that is being replayed day in and day out. We feel the love, and he likes to spend quality time together out in town and taking delight in me. It's not a fantasy of "this is what has to be done" feeling, and he is out of my life. If he knows there's something that needs to be changed, he is someone who will acknowledge it. It's just that with him, it has not been immediate. And I'm just irritated and to me, it's becoming a reality that this is who he is.

I haven't had many boyfriends in my life. Disappointments have me rendered not as sure, hoping to see what is called for. I have only been with a relationship physically, as a first experience, for no longer than two and half weeks, residing outside of my home state, to be clear, across the country and only to return home. Every day is going to be different than the day before. I can tell you the little addictions stayed in my mind regarding past fantasies or that life of the high life. In hindsight, the man who dealt strongly at first chose me, the female, who was addicted to love in all feeblemindedness. Almost all of me was taken apart with that one person who was not good for me and to be in my life. It took a long time to stop pondering about the past. My past that happened in my midtwenties.

All I know is, now I can see where my boyfriend extends his gratitude toward me. Whereas the other guy had no connection to me from the heart strings. The bad person for me wanted me for a passion of lust that required feelings and effortlessness. Sounds grand but no purpose or love behind this formula. Such as what if it didn't work. There was no explanation but to let me go. Truth was, I was the girl, the goal to get from, to get gone, and can only satisfy temporarily. This bad man never wanted to settle or even thought of getting married. Enough said. If God is love, and with God, all things are possible. Then maybe even love can be a trend for this person, but no, he is rather setting a trend, as if keeping contacts to do the same.

I'm pretty sure it seems odd as to why I would go into a relationship where the ducks are not all in a row. Whose perspective is it when I find a man who has his way all the time and can never stop, but is this true? No one knows. Is it my fault that I believe that and submit because this was not existent when I first met him, or do I? One can be perfect at first, then the hindrance shows up an alternate personality. I'm not saying ego. His ego is there all along, for everyone is entitled to an ego. I did not judge his personality getting in the way. It was more of his lack of communication. If I only knew this could be a deal breaker, but I was so consumed. I devoid myself of a right to an answer. At least in wholehearted commitment with Danny, I steered through the dark moments. My compass guiding me toward him. In dutifulness, he is stating he is a good man. With a bad person, I guess I would have to observe really carefully. I could pick up hints where it's, "What is this man trying to get away with." Maybe, I presume. That might've saved me a lot of trouble. I walked into it that one experience at age twenty-four.

A nice guy's personality can very much be a pursuit to romance, or instead, he tries to get my mind race on what topic he is set on because he has the better mood, which is all great. Everyone is a nice guy one way or another. It's all in managing the heaviness and flow I can handle, and what surprise am I able to take in. Would I have to console it painstakingly to the "attack" I never saw coming? I may feel relaxation in my spirit, that he's a good guy, not all bad. Though with that one share of experiences I had was a player and he looked at his own interests. I was not set up to decide. In my conscious-ness, I, as a naïve girl, was not ready. The evil curse once on me to have a lack of fear to do anything rash. Then in course, exhilaration condemning fear, as if unheard of, would be my "necessity" to act. When trafficked or being picked up, that moment was a factor of the ring leaders, seeing whether I was overwhelmed by the vigilance of life. Did I get overworked and did it all come crashing down? Steve Cohen stalked me. He knew what church I went to four years prior. Through process of stability, I healed from the shame that nudged me, but the guilt never attacked that much since it did the first time I had my virginity taken away. Though at times, it invoked sadness and unbelief to a slight extent. I just wanted to get on with life and see that past is done.

In contrast to those men, I see Daniel as a miracle also my counselor, to stop on by and drop off my trinket bong so a big deal. I must hold on to each day with a new outlook. Although I don't pine for it with a burdensome attitude, it just is. I try to fight the nega-tive attitude, summating it is a problem. I have found that the sub-stance found on the trinket had been of aqua green, and it was meth. Basically, liquid meth slathered on after being "confiscated" from me and being with that young man in the cocktail party like van where we had a one-day stand. What is special about the aqua color of the meth is that in 2006, I was twenty-six and had gotten in a psychotic breakdown. Where I was left with a solution of aqua-colored foam in bottle at an off-campus dorm and to never go back to. I went into a leave of absence that year from college. And now, it shows up eleven years later? Very interesting, yes.

Back to Daniel, he will be himself every day. I had this presumption that I could not oversee him being human. On the upside, all I have to do is relax. I can't control his next move. The whole picture defining that each ailment is to accept it as a benefit and not a loss. To check for it every day and be safe and regarded being in a right relationship. Life's not perfect. It's as if in mental illness, there's a break down or argument with him. Nothing is structured; anything goes. The element is how long is he going to stay mad and not how can I appease it more so. Who knows, I can try, but it can go so far. I've got to keep my mind intact foremost. Since it's hard to gather visible facts when in a break down. Regarding triggers, they are not exactly at the forefront always and easily obliged on the other hand. What's insufferable is to lead each other to be disappointed, and I'm saying both of us have distractions. There's got to be a way to say no. I will not get angry, and I will look at him like a companion. That is such a difference from the day I met him, and within twenty-four hours, we were boyfriend and girlfriend, physically. Yet he says we've met before, but I don't remember that brief chance encounter from years prior.

3
Chapter

Living with It

You may be thinking why would I choose my boyfriend, as I am a schizophrenic with decision issues, but then why would I not? I have suffered to know changes would come with a result, thus made by me, and some are only a bit quite unexpected. Having a label or diagnosis at the age of fourteen made me a totally complete opposite of who I thought I really am or wanted to be. To see a side of me where hope abounds has got to be on this earth. It'll have to be what I see while I live with my boyfriend. I don't experience bliss. I could be someone else for a lifetime, and now, who cares if I am a schizophrenic on earth? If I can believe, I don't base my judgments upon him as permanent as I feel others could do to me. He can change. I can change. Whatever the effort, the most I can do is work on myself. I try my hardest to stay stable, and sometimes, I am unaware that I may not be keeping in check my diagnosis.

By this, I mean I never say or remind the fact that schizophrenia has befell me. Neither do I judge a stranger until essential proof comes to mind, such as catcalling. And even then, at that, it's not an easy thing to think about for witnessing someone else also having symptoms. Maybe it's good to stay naïve, who knows. If there is such thing as apathy as being a perpetrator, I can believe it. I almost thought it was my psychosis that kept me in a rage, but my schizophrenia has a symptom or trait called apathy. No sympathy, empathy, guilt, or shame, and it drives the torture into my boyfriend. I am fully aware of my surroundings yet to get out of a situation, like an argument, is difficult because I feel deserving of love. We go at each other verbally until I hear the trigger, and then sometimes, I blow up where I can't handle how he brings the argument to no fruition. And then again, I don't either. These banished emotions; therefore, I want to get my frustrations across, but I don't see him qualified to communicate well also. And he probably is frustrated because he sees the same in me.

I've heard angering labeled as "schizo," being of verbal usage and expressed logistics because why say so much and go to that extent. I can go and describe myself crazy but why would I do that? Does that even suit me? How can such a label exist in continuance? If in jest, if for fun. Happiness should be, in all aspects, for everyone all the time. Utilization of "schizo," on the other hand, has been the contradictory term for playful; to be fair to describe the reality of life and its negative side, whether hereditary or by luck. Then to be affirmative, a lady is a lady, but she should not be called crazy either. Hmm. This is a cry out from the man to be heard, that he needs to be treated better. Name calling "crazy" may not be a weakness, but it is these small and rare circumstances, when it is a wakeup call, that it is to be withstood. With any other form to be held that it is, it can be misunderstood over and over again. Like with me, I hear "crazy" and "schizo" a little differently than others.

*****

My standpoint of females' behavior to the males is not established, yet I examine it as vitally true. I would immaturely concern myself about his past, meandering through possible answers as to why my man would consider being chased by a girl. Should I be worried? I am not aware of the exact situation at hand, but it does not mean it's a bad thing.

First of all, a woman does not experience the same struggles a man does. As a woman is created for a man, what would be the opposite of womanhood as toward growth? Would it be to trick a man (be a temptation) to hold him in a relationship hostage? Through sexuality, it wouldn't benefit both male and the female to get what she wants and then leave. I believe that isn't one bit innocent, especially when compared to an innocent man. If the man doesn't pursue, why is it for a man to mess the order for natural, societal rules? The man belittle and not capable to do his job to find the right woman for him. A man can be taken advantage of, no matter how little we hear that to be true.

Can I blame my man for not being patient? That would be illogical, but should I? Of course. When I was celibate, I was single, and I felt I was doing my job as a female. If he was not celibate, then he had an experience I know not well of. I take it as I didn't learn sex with just anybody. For him, was picking a girl that approached him being the one? Then again, two people sharing a social setting shouldn't turn them on to quickly cohabitating either. Particularly the reason being unconsciously fulfilling a desire without a real connection and pretending there is. Well, I say this, it takes two to tango. The naivete is that there are no evil women in this world. That is not true. All they need to do is stand up, rather than stand down, or is it? Do they know what they need to stand up to?

I wonder how someone is addicted to be in a relationship especially long-term. Well, that may be a given. To be obsessed is not blessed. I can tell I don't have all the goods one female can possess to have for their male partner. But I love him. I mean, in short-term relationships, it's the sharing of the bodies is getting what both parties wanted but to have each other being on the mind and heart? Is that of any importance? Does this afterthought exist? I see that it can when no one else occupies the heart; gullibly receiving sex. It is lonely without a spouse. Sex is a giving away of the body, stating it is not their own. To cherish sex or cherish the body (and purity therefore)? That is the question. Either you can love sex or hate yourself, but you can't have both to love until finding the one partner who will dedicate by doing the same. To give up the will, denying his body to stay exclusive, and only inclusive in body to me.

Now that I am along for the joyride, I mention no outsider can judge me as being deceitfully enticed. This is not the danger I'm escaping but an experience leading into the long run, and it can or it can't be exciting. That's personally my opinion and my choice. I guess in all my observation is that when it came to those that were a part of the trafficking, no one questioned so much, though I might have shared. It came down to, "Do I really want to be with Daniel?" And finally, it seemed different from the time the first experience rolled around back a decade prior. Back then, no one cared. If you care about Danny, then he must be something! Honestly, my mom cared about the first ever "boyfriend" too, but there was no denying I was on my way to the flight from Hawaii to the east coast to meet up with John.

Oh, she was persuading in letting me know if I've found the one and to make the right decision. I've made the mistake out of enthusiasm, a wrong state of happiness that had me choose wrong. With Danny, I knew that life was at hand. That choosing him meant maturity, unlike the past. Invalid encounters are not at all to be dismembered as negligent. When in all respect, there was no penetration. By this, I mean friends or those men I've dated without taking them home. I will remember to take that as a piece of me. I wouldn't have imagined I'd have dated men when I was a teenager. And look, I am no longer celibate. Hmmm.

How I don't want to wake up to that wicked person. And hey, maybe I'm not. I believe I'm not. To dwell on his past would be stupid. I only consider the truth to why we both have mood swings. Then to figure out on what would be the activity for the day. In my moments of high emotions stemming from what came as my boyfriend's repertoire of complaints or bad attitude, I have a lot to ponder myself. This continual ruminating, all of which turned out to negative energy on whether he should be my mate, come into play. I do not like it.

This is not what I want basically. I can tell, at the time, I don't want these thoughts or internal monologue to overtake my decision to be an impulsive, irrational bitch. Hardships once keeping me in a phase is my heart staying at a tight, cautionary place. I'm torn though with apathy. All I want to do is the right thing, if I could only think of a thing that could steer me. Am I foolish? No relationships are perfect they say, or there's more to what I've got to learn. And I have, somewhat. Anger is inherited in facial features and in receiving cues. As a child, that's how anger is defined, but as an adult, I can choose to respond differently. Even though "this for example" has once been a trigger I can opt out of aggression. Aggression is the result of anger. Anger is okay. Aggression not so much but can prevent it from happening before it starts. Hostility is an attitude. There is a difference between aggression and hostility. Hostility is ongoing, that is not very good at all.

As a schizophrenic in love, it takes me having to sit in front of my boyfriend or beside him to visually absorb or just take in his presence to have a peaceful time at home. I like home. This is when it's a furtive, quiet recollecting for me and him too, to be looking at our phones on the web or Facebook. All of a sudden, my guard gets snatched from beneath me. My solace turning into a consumption of ponderings of why I don't need this relationship. From this realm, I can then realize it's my fault for one, or do I? Since it is happening in my bubble or even within my personal zone. As if similar to taking a break, do I take my time when he's out of view? To have stretched out an answer to this dire inquiry, "Why him?" He may be thinking to himself, "Why her?" How about why must I choose a challenge in accordance to a relationship?

Don't delve into this energy! Should I say "time apart" as magic word? Why bother using a double standard to wasted energy when it could be useful. I know, waste no more time. It's best to get away as soon as possible, right? How can I easily convince myself to be in that mode and of gathering any totality of this abled man? He doesn't deserve the such to take an avenue to dwell in my mind. It is to no avail if I stay when all I want is progress. Why? For we both have an assumption/idea of "progress" in an argument. At times, I don't think I care what will hurt my boyfriend in the end. My motive in the near future is the "commitment to resolve." Can it be soon with a good dosage of the right medicine and the right atmosphere? I desire nothing but enjoying the moments with him in happiness. Any appearance of hindrances I would like not. Any dependencies when I should leave well be, or do I despise? Am I finally getting over that? I hope so. Yet how familiar it is giving into glee, as it is freeing since it is the comparison rather. Opposed to the heartbreaking resonance that protruded so in the initial stages of our relationship in living together.

Should I tell him how I'm feeling, or give it a try? But my emotions flare, then at times, I try to take accountability. I show what to be aware of when the hate has dissipated. My internal monologue repels any acknowledgment that he has emotions too. I have a choice. In fact, on top of that, he needs to know I appreciate his presence, and I respect his bubble. It's worth it, every time he needs for me to coddle his feelings with a thank you and/or quality time. It is easy in giving in, to doing things together when the momentum has started. Is it the magic of having a good day or morning that makes it happen? Or could it be the choice of someone and how to deal with that decision factor every day since the consummation started? The stress utilizes my weakness. In all entirety, it can be overcome the next day, or when it needs be, with no problem, but then the following morning, I wake up to a partner. Do I incoherently say I deserve more by pursuing a course that is really nonexistent? Does it make sense to figure out whether I'm blinded to the present and what or who should be cherished? *Yes!*

For a mentally ill to act out in definitive proportions, isn't it funny a wavelength is needed to be just enough to tolerate? And what is this wavelength thingy? Can't I accept my ideas and way of thinking as final and not have to give in to permission, to not have them be stepped on because it's not "part of his lifestyle?" What choice is there for motivation in myself? My will power fancies solace, to fill up this space only emotion can fill. What would be this emotion, varying in cause of eliciting patience to announce communication purposeful? Yet my bipolar diagnosis leads me to a mania.

My mindset tells me I can "handle this," almost convening to an order, but never assured of the thought processes leading to an affirmation. I'm fine one minute, but with the disturbed outlook is the opposite on the spectrum. And this is the depressed part of a bipolar disorder. With my boyfriend, I attempt to speak regularly to get a detail across, but it shone more to unnecessary than unfruitful. Since what I have is a regulation to never explain too far. I suppose I don't have much to say. On account of him, maybe I'm oblivious to the fact that he does listen.

To be put at ease, my energy is used to voice my assumed corrected version of sanity. Nothing short of checking off my guilt for my crazy conversing. At other times, well maybe, all the time, I want to ask, "why such the matter?" This must be why he tends to have me realize that peace and guilt come hand in hand. Conviction is something he deals with, yet at the same, he is not aware of and neither am I. He's almost blaming me to take it into account, an issue that I don't even, at the time, realize. Then I see it to be him needing healing from a hurt.

There are times when I kind of want to remove myself from a gathering. It isn't easy when I don't feel at home or when I am not feeling sociable. Then again, I grew up shy. I'm familiar with shyness, and it'll show up seen and loathing. The memories of more often walking away from a scene with my boyfriend is abundantly plain. I'm sorry to him that I wasn't there for him at those times. It was difficult to think I would be handling him, and it won't work out. And then, there is this taunting, that what I'm doing is visibly awkward. And then, what he really needs is love, but I get paranoid, like he's only doing this to embarrass me.

Then I get upset, and I direct it at him to be a release of my irritation. He wanted to encounter my love in a weird way. Yes, perhaps, and I could've submitted to his aim. I cared what other people thought a little too much, and my boyfriend calls it, "Paranoia will destroy you." Maybe I've embarrassed him because the excuse was, he should show more attention to his girlfriend. He's a little on the manic side himself too. I must really have high expectations on my boyfriend, that I felt intimidating subcurrents whenever I was in public because I want to take pride in someone. I decided him to be a long-term boyfriend/significant other unlike any. A little part of me was depressed of having no use for socializing, and importantly, I see myself having no ability to at that time. Using logical calculations that have me readily available and not deemed having mental afflictions, did I see myself turning into development brewing. Conducive to the withdrawing phases I had in hindsight, I can't change them, but the right choice is to not turn back any way.

The definition of insanity as someone taken from a mental institution and seen doing the act of something over and over again and expecting different results. As opposed to someone in society, perhaps. How do I see no backing to the proof that the insanity cannot apply to a stable yet disabled, diagnosed mentally ill individual? How is he/she labeled insane by being put in a box for having no goals or any ambition? I mean, if it concerning actions only, I guess that would be the matter all in good taste to describe insanity, intentions aside. No one "wants" to do something over and over again, or would they be expecting "what result?" How would I know that I was doing something over and over again? That would not be fair to call me insane for being able to seek help. It would seem my personal relationship would have no necessity of observational data except to hold the title of *insane.*

Is insanity confirmed the fact no one knows why anybody would do the same thing over and over again? I see where stupidity starts. I stopped where it could've started. I sense that reality in others, I should see it more in myself, I suppose. The mentally ill person, like me, may have an impediment rendering. Like me, unable to recognize my decisions, perhaps temporarily. Maybe not even able to mind my loved one's reactions or thoughts on the matter at hand, but instead, I just go for it. I go for the jugular.

The theory of minding no one is big to me. It's like apathy. It states, "without a care if the public are there, yet if only they cared." And that's the public realm delving into the paranoia and apathy leading to home. Its starts as cameras, then I believe in this house I'm safe. I feel more like apathy has its serene way of getting my needs met. When Danny speaks, I have no inclination to respond. I may have one sentence at hand, but it doesn't seem to be viable. At first to me, then I believe, he won't like it either. Am I clinically insane to getting what I want and the struggle therein? But what is it that I want? To get a further explanation on what would be the different result? Because really, this describes anybody with so-called objective functioning in society.

This is an impossible but valid argument to a normally fated person. When this place of remoteness is replaced and security is not enough, I want a different result. When I go through episodes, wouldn't I like to get back to reality? And give it one more try? Will I turn out normal without these outbursts? I don't want to live with schizophrenia, yet on the contrary, I need to overcome the challenges of my disease. Outbursts on to my boyfriend are a part of it. I don't want that, I desire better. Heartlessness shoved in my face; I can't do nothing about it. To a healthy person like me, I hope insanity is short-term.

I choose to help myself by living life and luckily, get out of demonic possession. I choose not to get locked up in an institution by doing obstructive accommodations over and over again. I know I need to change (and grow). I presume an outsider uses the term *insanity* to label someone not like them. Can anyone describe what I'm doing verbally and physically as insanity? An internal switch doesn't turn on to control or stop myself toward thinking positively, or does it? I bypass the degree of resolution, when the external stimuli of unfriendly people and internal stimuli cannot be attested for.

I instead hold my peace. I invent no solution to have banter. There is no careful undertaking there. Altogether with resistance, is the level of fake facades and personalities. Yet schizophrenia is more than anger venting. It is also suffering the various components of symptoms and torturing progressive or degressive developments in atmosphere. I can't restrict or mandate what gets to stay the same. It's like I tell doctors something new every decade that passes. Subliminally, I'm saying, "I can't do anything about it." Sadly, I can't say it loud enough. In irony, the doctors already know.

To find the definition of love for me was in accordance to my terms and standards, all in memory or what can be derived from the other person. I absolutely respond though. How can I tell myself I heard something if I don't know I really heard it? The cry in my head urges me to believe in continuing faith about him. And then I hear, "It'll get better."

The outcome has to be me abiding importance in what he has to say. This has already turned in to a difficulty for me to approach him. When I made my decision to avoid him, my continuance to stay away had become more of the priority I dreamt about. In a nutshell, my ignorance toward him had to be all or nothing. One day, I grab my notebook and start writing, and my boyfriend comes up to me and says, "Focus on the positive, not the negative." I guess we both need affirmations. I can't seem to get my words out with harshness. I'm nitpicky, and my anger doesn't take labels too well, so my fists have spoken before. I don't get it. Is it my fault? Must I get used to the fact that how I feel may never end?

I react to what he says, unsure of the stimulus behind his words, yet all this time, he was loving me. His pursuits were all in innocence, but golly, it's not an easy task to decipher, or being convinced, he's about to attack with an insult. Is it because I have no idea that I'm picking up on a certain uneasiness from a part grudge or setback? Perhaps my ignorant father? Danny is a human being with human nature. If not only, at least, a man has ways. How else in the world can one decline? I am also a being of ways of my own. I cannot program him to converse on the spot with a snap of my fingers or set a timer showing when I am more secure to receive on my schedule and to my liking.

*****

There's a reason schizophrenia is called a mental illness. For symptoms of ongoing torture that has happened upon initial diagnosis. It had me silenced with no validity to whatever explanation could it be and to what was going on in my mental experience and exhaustion. How can this get better or at least more consistent with ease or some sort of consolation? All I started doing was taking the antipsychotic medicine at age fourteen. So I freaked out and had outburst against my parents, which had me sent by a squad car to the shelter for misbehaving kids. There, the social worker asked if I heard voices and thought if people could read my mind. I said, yes, for the heck of it. Next thing I knew, my dad is in the youth psychiatry office with me and the doctor. Was that necessary for my dad to give in to the doctor without giving me the courtesy to ask if I was suffering a mental illness? I trusted too much in authority at a young age, like most youth, and I went with the flow. In history class in high school, I couldn't keep my head up, and I would drool pools of saliva onto the desk. I could barely hear what the teacher had to say. "Wah, wah, wah, wah."

It was a blur, and my body felt it too as my mind managed to think what my next class was and where do my feet start walking to now.

What I feel is a great regimen to hold my thoughts accountable, and it is to ask, "Do I need to mull this over in my mind?" Right? Is it in submission to love because I have asked myself enough to let go of the hate? I assume if I have to think it over and over, it isn't worth ruminating over, no? Whatever is it about my boyfriend, I can't seem to think of there being anything ceasing. Such as in the concept of who he is. He is misinformed by my standards and of what is in my brain. That I am the one truly taking hold of the irregularity. It happens a lot when he's not around me, then to give into my own impressions, however, not true.

It is where I get lost in the condoning of him and not celebrating him. I ought to celebrate me. The essential break from what he has to say is refreshing. What he observed was "wrong" was "so Jeannie." Why don't I fix my habit? It kind of revives my soul taking his side again. All right, I'm slow. I need to catch up. I forgot to make life for us tolerable. To look into that, nothing big. He's never used those words, "to make us tolerable," at me. I look into the part how it's irking my mind to formulate an exceptional idea of a partner most of the time. If he fits it, great. No matter how surreal, it's only rebellious, and the reality pans out. Do I take it to keep my psyche on the up and up? No! I have responsibilities to heal from my past. Unresolved feelings unearthing is the reason I get so catty.

Have I ever ruined the day by making him clean up my mess, removing my love all the while the crime was whose? I'm always cleaning up his. I take his word, and I aggravate on that that my mood is destroyed. I blame him. I surveyed his heart, and my conclusion is this—he is swayed by his need for me to care so much. I apologize to him in how I attempt to accuse him of disrespecting me.

Schizophrenia can be a sort of brand between positivity and negativity. If the good is seen, it's more of a neutrality though. I sometimes feel a realm is required of me. Don't get me wrong. I have displayed disdain and harsh treatment it would seem to others. Probably an infliction due to being closed-minded, but I have been told I am just a baby. Though in my indiscretion as a teenager, I have definitely lashed out like a bad seed at home to my parents and brother.

Now, it's like the remnants of defects has produced once again for my boyfriend to grapple. The healthy goodness with my diagnosis, schizoaffective disorder, is that I have held a job and did my best to be courteous. That one ability to enjoy life can be thwarted by different circumstances from life-altering decisions. By changing a bad outlook to good, now heavy a description, can I give on how fed up he must've been? I can't. I just need to move on with no reflection, and why? Because at this moment, the apathy is pretty effective at this present stage, yet I tend to roll with it. Coupled with depression, only slight, and the hopes of a wonderful future. Do I know he has a bad outlook? What does it matter but for us to benefit from each other, emphasize symbiosis? Yes, it's another word for helpmeet. Together, we work out.

Even I have processed my thoughts but I have questioned if the certainty of an option was laid out before me. I'm holding onto these inhabitant synapses contributing to my confusion, or am I thinking fast to lose control? My impulses empowered in return to answer with, "How is this the low road taken? Did I end up in mania?" This must be the bipolar side of me. My schizoaffective is driven from a delusion-related force, when at those unstable periods in life. It looks like I have a mission to pursue or on crazy forth from a false belief. Stating being psychotic in relationship is difficult. Self-righteous justification has bloomed from the irritability turned monster. I resort to calling my psychosis to be on the streets or in public. The extremities being enough to look back and say that was psychotic and out of sorts. There are those grandiose delusions being blindly volunteered on by me. I have no idea these are downright inconceivable. These are unheard commitments to be carried on in the society. Am I catering to people watching? No, this is top secret. I'm being facetious.

It's not quite a voice, but it is a flash direction of a will to act all from this internal expectation: "I better get to it, now go!" Life must go on, and I must justify what an independent trance that set me on to what needs to be done. I could be walking an avenue to fulfill some sort of an end mission. And all the while, during the stroll, is no idea set on anything else. I believe that until the "project" is complete. I, then, "hear" the next flash of the command; I stop where I am at to get to work on leaving out of scene that I am at now. Boy, would I sure give anything to be convinced there's got to be a way to make it easier and to find what else I should be doing next.

My last psychotic breakdown, I should've seen coming. I developed a thinking of a negative inner monologue. Giving my two cents out loud in my head. More so pertaining to the harsh, critical treatment I've been experiencing by customers at work and sometimes, outside of work to make matters worse. How can I cope by gradually eluding from reality and ultimately trusting in God? Reality to grasp were manners and courtesy, and then, how can I relax? Working full-time and part-time jobs. Along with the forgiveness and forgiving, I have to do overall. This bantering in my head is confronting me and is dependent on how calm I am at the time. Then I choose to respond externally to the other person. I once appeared to maintain a resignation. The volume of "let it go" and not do what I feel has made me laugh out loud so to speak. Actually, it hasn't. I felt like I've been stripped of my freedom to enjoy my employment. Did I want to laugh out loud? Oh, laugh harder and louder! If that would explain things but I couldn't just do that. It has happened one phase in my midtwenties before my virginity was ravished away.

Some may think how did my boyfriend choose me? He had past relationships. I resolve it to be that he must not judge all women to be the same. There must be wonders of women he finds attractive, though in me, it feels right. I believe his exes are the ones that put blinders on him, a good man, and giving him the perception that to have a worthless relationship is a lifestyle tolerable to him. Strong to face something like that yet how daring. Unbeknownst to him, he was being taken for granted, and though it may seem a time for celebration, I have a hunch the subconscious could see right through them. No offense, they could've meant no harm. It's just the blatant squander of time with a stable man I reckon. He should have a great companion to see him through at least. I'm not as smart as them, or am I?

God sees the situation more than me, so there you have it. I can say no more. I didn't expect to have a relationship as different as I had imagined. I have gotten down to pat an alternate universe to deal with when on some of those days, I have, on occasion, tensed up. What's worse is that I find myself looking unconsciously angry, and it drives me insane that I don't care. Regardless for him or me, the pessimist or schizo in me should be resisting to want to see the sad story because it's difficult to find the fairy tale. Can't he want me like a real boyfriend wants their girlfriend or vice versa? I ponder. It's just me, huh? I dwell no longer how I was a girlfriend for the two years we've been together.

At low points in my day, I have flashes of doubt in any improvement. More so, my thoughts say I am unable to counteract my mood swings. All of a sudden, I'm at my wit's end, fighting for happiness and peace again. All to have no capacity to worry. An argument hasn't emerged. I'm only by myself. It's the perfect time for the demon to work me up, I think. I am thankful for my boyfriend. I see the struggle of humility and that he chooses to go out of his way, which is so manly. Is it self-condemning to have him top gun over my life?

If I tried to sustain through my own independence with my strength at this point, without him, it would be exhausting. Couldn't I be doing better? Do I think I can dive into what I'm doing without him, just like the days passing? And I needed to space out more than keep myself busy? I'm kidding yet partly true. I am tired of not knowing what to do. When he tells me to be on target and wrap my head around the situation at hand as "part" of reality, I cringe. Truth being, I'm not an object. I'm a human being, so why am I fearing the life of living what's ahead? And this should be practiced. I'm still grateful.

The definition of *passion* to me is I've found him. My heart says, "I want to stay with him." I've had struggles telling me the negatives of having to be with him. There would be no hope, the voices would tell me. Receiving that, I'd hear myself say, "I don't want him." But I still kept doing life with him. Our passion equaled the drive to stay together, even though he never understood the concept of courtship, at least, when it came to me. Of course, this view had to change. Over time, the idea of "I am the one for him" came to mind and felt like, well, that's better than nothing or "forget about it, I don't like him." A solid foundation of our whatnot "courtship beginnings" has to be the constant outlook of positivity that maybe it did happen. Because in retrospect, the confirmation of passion became real when the change was now our future being together. That being evident of the two becoming one, by having us live together in a homeless transition shelter and signing both our names to stay there as a couple. Our first shelter, besides the campus bathroom.

I take the scripture in the Bible that says, "Better to marry than burn with passion." This is meant for me and him, regarding the worse has come upon us. If it weren't for my boyfriend, I could've chosen the wrong person or that 'one' because my unstable state or condition kept me looking for love. I don't feel like I've been misguided. Whatever doubts, the introduction was to be in contact full form. I've recalled saying, "It's the final state. We'll know in the end."

It's an even statement. With love most uncandid, I can try to reach out to the listener of the story we had. I can tell one of frustration now. Of what could be, I cannot attain to being pretentious or prideful of the prosperous sort, and by that, I mean, however, you'd like to take it in an extreme case. We do get by though. I tell myself to cope with him in public, and the choice I must make is to not cry out in sheer embarrassment. I want to receive his help, and I'm hoping its more help than destroying. I desperately try to fend away ideas that he really wants to irritate me. My boyfriend must be a real, great performer. The way he goes all out to have me on my feet and in continuity, motioning me to respond or react to my issue. I say yes, a lot. His dubiousness to this constant idea disturbs me as well. I can't be saying yes *all* the time.

When love aligns, it feels like I've gone out of my way. Does he not know it? I may get sad at first, then I see him respond in lieu of my devotion. That makes me happy. He must have quality time as a love language, or the way I said something made him feel acknowledged. The truth of the circumstance is—my love is true, he is true. He truly cares about how I treat him, and he cares and loves me. He thinks of me as worthy. I am thankful I can be aware of this. I see the sensitive side of him.

Likes and dislikes are one way to extend myself from the paranoia I hear. When I don't like what my boyfriend said, I tend to disengage inwardly by expressing outwardly and immediately. Boy, I am quick with the tongue as if the liking is no longer, and the dislike has gone further. And now the idea to attack seems logical, without thinking the reciprocation seems so necessary. Easily reachable. Then again, it can't be bad really. These are the times I need to gauge. It may be his turn to state what he hates. It's not a big deal, but in real life, it is.

These blowups can be a manifestation of his or my past hurts. The safer one feels in a relationship and loved, only then do the emotions that need to be healed arise. Little misunderstandings tend to look bigger, needing every effort to douse with vengeance. But no need for that. Instead, look to the source of what made it seem like a big deal. He is not asking, "Why do I do this?" I need to fix myself at this point since he has no intention to push a relationship away. I have no right to use a scepter in judgment. It'd be altogether selfish. What he said had come too easy, and I feel sad and ashamed that it had to be that way.

I had downfall within my reach if, at a vicinity, I didn't have someone to be with. It could be anyone I choose wrong in my life. No matter if he's a man and what age that looks mature, if the heart doesn't suit my personal space, then he could be a man with intentions with polygamy. Me and Danny's bubble became "one" into *our* bubble and letting go felt detrimental. If it weren't for him, I'd be back into the habit of aimlessly saying yes to a wicked man, wanting to take advantage, and even part of a prostitution ring. Daniel was not one of those men. He seemed approachable with a desire and wonder, not by necessity and danger, feeling like it's this or else.

Unlike other relationships where most people get to know each other before committing themselves in marriage, it was not so much the case with me and Danny, we didn't exactly date before pledging dedication to Danny. It was because I had friends, and I was stable, at one point, with an independent lifestyle. I got by like a student who just graduated from college. If that makes sense, I wanted to look like I made it, at least, with better-looking clothes or to be on the up and up but in a quick minute. There was a time I needed to start over with getting clothes during college because of a psychotic breakdown and a restraining order (such a hubbub). And then on the good note, having employment had me buy clothes. My mom gave me some nice garments too, and sure, I missed them when I had to get over them. I'm back to square one with none of those. When I showed up in Danny's life, I was wearing the same outfit for many days. Apart from him looking at the outer appearance, I believed singlehood had been important to him, but now, allowing love to find him, he found much clarity. I'm glad he took the time out for us to hang out the day we met in 2017, or at least, he invited me to join him. We were in a slight rut, so to speak, and fate has us meet again, never to part or separate this time.

I agree being "in love" is synonymous with infatuation. I've had that "in love" feeling with extremity, only to find that person never was for me. Life fulfillment with each other wasn't that guy's interest. He forsook the truth with my body, careless to the fact that an engagement means forever. It's that misunderstanding turned into a mistake. I mean, how long does it take to respond from lust? And then to figure it's okay to take my virginity? With my procedure done from the STI's during homelessness, after twelve years of being sexually transmitted diseases free except for the human papillomavirus from John, I now had two more for a duration of less than a month. I feel like I've suffered more than having been consumed by the 'fallen in love" state. Each day felt difficult experiencing a once happy elated moment. Until of course, I submitted to the fact I had to forget somehow in order for things to be better. Or at least for the most part.

Before becoming a live-in couple with Danny, it had been a bit of survival, and it was spiritually taxing. The holding on to life and moving on is always on the back of the mind, but for that time, and maybe even now, it's like I'm following a moral code or a certain path I'm on. I wasn't suicidal, yet I needed more help than the psych ward allotted I'd tell myself. Seeing the whole picture and how we moved to another state less than a year later, I can now only hope for the best and a wonderful healed outcome. In all respects to the change, I couldn't see regret forming. The heartbreak that didn't show itself had got me rarely looking back. I had one heart wrenched mourning session, full of loud sobs, hoping it had cleared my need for healing. I was proud of my decision. I was crying now because the story behind it was supremely non-reliant to who I thought I'd be. Enthusiasm forwarding the tears was that this is my life now, mistakes in it and all. I tried not to be cowardly, but I couldn't help myself. These would be the days where all I could think of are any and all "red flags" I may have missed whether deliberately, foolishly, or decisively.

Maybe I got to know Danny for the years I've stayed with him. I have wondered with forbearance if I'm supposed to be with him. By accepting him, there must be a change coming or to celebrate him more. Is there something about cohabitating? That it has to be steady for a year or two because ours had been volatile. It seems the answer is in the comparison of the stats of men available now. Where are they? And when they were there, why not? That's the reply to why Danny. Because there is no one like him. I can tell monetary compensation can guide me into a new relationship, but it does not have to be the final guide into choosing the one I do or don't believe.

On the topic surrounding hardships and nowhere to start, wanting to try with him is a battle to comprehend him or winning it on behalf of me. It's like a trait in me to have this emphatic designation to, in little words, tell him, "You're going down!"

Yes, he must be overtaken. My sincerity is overrun, incapable to delve in the conviction to give up and then give love. I think it's sad that I skip past the "opportunity." If it weren't for him though, I could be wandering around, aimlessly looking for a way to survive or run into trouble. Someone like him in my life is clearly the piece of help sent to me. Doing this alone with my early morning grasp of motivation is not an easy task. I agree with this, seeing he devoted himself to make his way into my surroundings. He is a life partner, even though it's my decision, and my decision can only break apart my relationship. Others would allow it if it were to better my life or because I deserve better in their opinion. Wouldn't that sole choice be on my head? And that is so true, but why do I feel like if I did, they could care less in the end? Of course, anyone can settle for more than who is at the moment. Then how come it's about slandering the said person as if they "know?" Those are technically a pondering or thoughts out loud, I'm pretty sure there's not a means to talk bad.

Monogamy is the wholesome proposal for me to cohabitate with him. I have come to realize that I must state that to Danny and have him become aware of my standards for equipage. It's the same view with him. Monogamy can equate marriage in the long run, even though his proposal to marry me had always been casually carried about. To dwell on personal matters never come into play because reality is, they are readily accessible for conversation to a stranger but how foolish would that be? Reckoning on the personal peace I can have, the quiet calm still has me moved to think about the complaints we've outdone ourselves with. With time, the notion of weight upon weight had gotten lighter, but it isn't almost delightful when men or my boyfriend senses my insecurity and makes me hold it accountable. Different as I am, I must've been open to show my insecurities. I attempt to tell him I don't want to be offensive, and I am wanting to understand, that we both know I am insecure, what can I do about it? "Do my artwork," he says, "because that's my hobby." I spend my time with art. It has been a huge help to see the prettiness in my creation. I can't say it keeps me exactly calm, but it does keep me grounded. There are "other" daily activities, but I can't lose my creativity.

Is there a subconscious in knowing it's not going to last, when I'm on such a roll by joining a drawing class? How my mental force exclaims this too will cease? What an ingrained composition I possess. I do not like to rewire my brain, undoing the figuring of whether this is all temporary. And sure, enough COVID-19 era shows up. Classes are cancelled at the specific location, and my set appointment to display my artwork is on hiatus. It can be that way for me and a hobby, I move on. Monologues, on the other hand, I had this spark of energy for, and then my phone shuts down with lack of storage. And no matter how many times I erase a file, I run into a problem.

*****

I'm a schizophrenic. When it comes to the force I must work with and through the realm called symptoms, never doubting, it keeps me in the zone of the supernatural. It is when I don't know how to love and show affection in a situation as called for. This is seen, though not from a prerogative or a personality to withdraw but the effect of apathy. I take on a false pretense of responsibility to triumph over problems with ideas and thoughts, rather than compassion and loving emotion. When single, I can have the motive to be bubbly and entertain coworkers, if needed be, and seem like a normal citizen. I was able to seem normal like I had no illness. But with a relationship, it takes a toll and effort beyond what I'm used to. I have to relearn compassion and go to the next level, which is pretty much a praiseworthy task. God must think I'm honorable, but I feel like I'm failing.

In jest, I want to say to my boyfriend, when he reminds me I'm schizophrenic that, "Well, at least you're getting through to me."

The determination if only received either way. Not enough for me to process, though no explanation is needed there. I feel he has made up his own method from some part of his brain. "A sturdy alternative" in how to treat me but in all relevancy, I'm not an alien. I had normal friends. The desecrated nothing of the first meeting being conducive to a relation of friendship. I must mention that I hadn't admitted off the bat that I had been a schizophrenic. I'm sure along the way the fact became known through the grapevine perhaps. In all frenzies, social medias are the thing to work with. This brings me to my next point, how do people in general distinguish mentally ill so symptomatic that they're dangerous or extreme?

I'm sure someone has to have the best exposure; therefore, knowledge on what a mental illness is, for example, "hearing voices." How did talking to voices become an entertaining ridicule? And I'd ask the question of, "How is that possible? To talk to an enemy to get rid of them. Or worse, to believe it can be done from a distance or not?"

I talk of enemy as to speak of the "person" behind the voices as if they have a soul and an intent to distract me with their audible "words" perse. Who is to say talking aloud is to get rid of the voices because why not? The answer may be a myriad to some, but from a genuine mental condition, it's not out of maliciousness. To express hearing voices, maybe a frustration, all the while knowing these sources are not people. The suffering of audio or visual hallucinations to the point of extremity is not a limit to decipher. A normal person's limit cannot be anymore known to a psychiatrist as than a freshly diagnosed schizophrenic. To find out, is there going to be more taunting by individuals who really ought to exercise self-control?

Anybody, literally, most normal healthy beings can let go of a memory by an affirmation to themselves in the moment to distract present inklings to reminisce. Why am I afraid like I would snap? All right, I am normal enough to let go of a memory that I don't want by working on a hobby, but has it been easy? No! And just because I let out a whisper in no shape or form am I requesting an answer or hopefully not. Time has made me believe this. To reshape my addiction of heartbreak and move on when there is no opportunity left and see where it leaves me. I am no longer in need of that memory. Good riddance. It's sad how stereotype has made me look like I can achieve hearing a character or voice talking back.

And if so, is it audible or in my head only? If it's from a random loud voice to get feedback, I'd rather disregard it though. Listening in on a piece of "sureness to get an answer" out of nowhere, I can, but to that effect, it would consider me delude reality. It would expound full effort to reach a nonexistent result over and over again, and wouldn't this be insanity? Don't you think? Let's just say, I know when to drop it or in obliviousness, how it naturally faded. Well, good for me if I knew before it happened (being facetious). What I'm getting at is other priorities got me going, but my mental illness brings up something. An allure of the "silliness of this one time," and it had been a defining leverage to talk about it and to "let go" at the same time.

Mental illness was never fun and games. If I had an auditory hallucination whether from inside the house or outside and/or someone stating brashly my "status," he may not even be a real person. And my brain had imagined it only. All in all, it has a derogatory and condemning tone for being in the house or staying in. Telling me, it hates me.

4
Chapter

Keep at It, Maybe?

How about if I told you that to fall in love, it takes me a clean slate. To have already begun to free myself from whatever selfish state that the heart has become. Apart from the "look at me" running toward status quo, screaming, "I need a boyfriend." I needed none of that, or did I in finality? My hormones were declaring "Fulfillment please," but I was filled with regret with my first experience ironically. In retrospect, I guess I had no moral compass to figure out a prerequisite to a satisfied lifestyle. And then, achieving the solution by jumping into what seemed to be the "man of my dreams." And I must have been mistaken learning from life's lessons. I have no intention to chase after a status in a man, when in self-introspection to him, I had none of my own. Yes, again, silly me.

Above all, it takes forgiveness because a relationship is one and done when this one's done. "Forget about that guy," I have been told plenty of times. My shortsighted evaluation on it was, "How can it be over?" Will I get it finally? Will I swallow the truth? That bitterness and grief were unnecessary, yet it still is to process my trauma. Ultimately, slight negating mattered in his reality, to this John Doe. Especially how he wasn't there to process with me or ask, "How am I doing, really?"

*****

When it came to disputes with my boyfriend, what happened was pure negative energy, and I handled it wrong. Even as vengefully as I could, I believe I deserved more. Nothing had gone perfect in how I expected fights as couples would go. A hint of appropriation of any sort would do, to tell me goals were needed. Whatever goal, if it were, I don't feel the need to give up the acceptance of him calling me schizophrenic. I'm milling it over, and in summation, I know that it wouldn't end. It would be insane to think otherwise. The anger had been surreal, but it's better to accept there'd been no change. No matter how effectively communicated he dismissed it from the start and then some. His bantering makes me believe it's my fault that I'm schizophrenic, or it's a fault of someone else's. I wanted to relate that this avenue of fighting, I don't see the use of it.

Apparently, me correcting him gets him sensitive and over fluxed. I did him wrong that he can't get over it. I hope he doesn't hold a grudge. If my complaint was valid, I guess it doesn't have to be. He has such a backdrop that he wants to get out and that mine doesn't need to be heard. "I am the one." Sounds good, given he's already there. Rather than, "I don't want him" and that doesn't sit well with me. The day I met him was the day I had to spend well. I didn't have a chance to ruminate through my emotions. The day to hang out with him for the first time, I had been drawn to the feel of ease. I tried so hard to pick up on his cue, and it was at every moment, nonetheless, that what we needed to do is agree. We now have all the time in the world.

All being said, I have a bipolar boyfriend and not a schizophrenic one. His condition derives from the giving of mental reckonings turned outward into mania. I've come to think he has a knack for psyche forewarnings or reacts on his anxiety toward a certain thing. Any explanation to come forward with that is a nil. He really displays energy or shuts down with lack thereof. Funny thing is, it looks like he doesn't stray from displaying knowledge in social settings, yet he has social anxiety disorder. I think for a male schizophrenic, it would be worse to choose freely in social settings or easily be comfortable in them. The diagnosis of schizophrenia is in how the suffering is unbearable, that one could tell I can't behave normally. Danny, on the other hand, thrives on attention. I see where the affliction is not so bad in a schizophrenic, when it is more for the good. When I, for example, can deflect the voice in having ruin my life during a psychosis, I as a schizophrenic experience paranoia, a symptom pertaining to "thought" and the uncontrollable aspect of it having them run would have me a bit fearful. From having a diagnosis and the far cry of coping skills not working is the rare result of catatonia. It resembles a lot like "denying thoughts."

The reason of someone realizing their duty to the other is because of love through dedication. To daily care for me, conveniences easier could've been. And in finality, I lost a lot, but my hope is up. I have a bipolar boyfriend. Me and Danny are doing life together. But Danny is not a sociopath. The observation of his loved ones and how he cared for them came into play. They say less good about him because they know I must face him, and what I see is what I get. I wonder if they despise his inkling toward self-glorification and have some grudge, but it's not really from him. The obsession to have people see him as king, I wonder if he keeps hidden. If I do, I am thankful he can keep me grounded by having him as authoritative in making his concerns count.

When it comes to each other, we were calling it a boyfriend/girlfriend relationship, then husband/wife though by chance. And the concept never really was, safe to say, heard again. The concern to me is that I don't want to lose him because I hurt him, and then, the feelings of hate have me sense a "justified resistance," like I'm right to take my stand. I don't want us lingering on a momentary life story, but sometimes, I want to be sure of my future, one day at a time. I suppose there are different ways a person or each individual grasps life. If he isn't the one, I still need to have the future happen, and of course, it's an agreement and not by using each other. All's fair in love and war. I don't know if he knew we were for each other or not, but we were together to get where we needed to go.

Call it the universe's plans, but I set out to love God from the start. I refuse the universe's plans, be it so broad to refute between a match like ours. I submit to God in continuum, to supply a life as far as I know never parting ways. I can't realize at present, but I am coming close to accept the clock. It has been set in motion to have a "first live-in" boyfriend. Be it at least two years to flip upside down the world I lived in, compared to when I was single.

Prelude to Poems and Conclusion

I write my poems not from a view of wanting to be fake, no, instead from a woman's view of holding an ideal of love in her life. A vision if you will, yet I cannot comprehend the emotions it takes to really understand what I write. I am still able to pen it out. For what it's worth, I had been a creative writer in my elementary school years. My English teacher in middle school called me out of my history class to tend to her class and read my story because it stood out to be an example. I can't believe I have that memory of age thirteen, and what possibly could I have come up with as a story for her assignment?

I wrote about my boyfriend to have me believe I am supposed to be with my boyfriend. That I am in God's will, even when I have apathy, and the relationship has been a narcissistic mess. And now, we come to the sad part of this story but in a good way. It's the end that makes sense or at least has to. With almost three and a half years to stay "in love," I am, for the most part, out of it. Times are getting better. I have to strive through each day and be thankful and humble to be alive. He had an addictive personality, which I still won't mention what, and that I have had enough. I can't handle it anymore. A human being in my life should be a blessing out of love and understanding, and I must believe I deserve [and not have to grasp] that piece of sunshine.

His saving my life ended up us being together. The addiction led it away from God. It could've been good, but his faith in this world was short, and that is a difficulty he or I was not able to take on. Maybe one day it'll all be good, but this could either have been an unfixable personality or a hopeful future of us being best friends in heaven.

At this moment in a shelter, it has been two days since I last spoke with him. I have my friend who helps me with this heartache as she has gone through trials herself. "I've gotten the chance to love someone," she said. That's true. And that's why it hurts. The awakening moment. Because of me, he'll have eyes opened, that he must now make a change. Sounds swell.

Being in love must really blinded me. It blinded me because I never got to see who he really is. Pushing away the hurt is like pushing away the confidence of "who he is," as I want to hold onto. Maybe there is a side of him I do know. But I'm making sure that I'm "not sure," and that is just fine to not try to assemble inklings. There is no any side of him for me, and this keeps me sane.

In this world of going through the motions of relations or even friendships, it looks like I "learned" the flesh is one hardship to escape.

What I say to calm the soul is when alone to invite that negative energy. Or at least, don't push it away. If it's a very necessity that is correcting you, then let it scream out. If it brings pain, then use other coping skills, like taking a walk. Look within your borders, if only for a second, because we can't escape every negative thought. Try not to avoid a piece of energy, just a piece, be it negative, to help you.

Basically, it guides me by saying, I can either get through this or master the comparison by what I can change or keep. Negative energy is the means by which we keep moving and judge ourselves. Please, no more wishing for the up and up and waiting for the present to be "here." Since the surroundings are here! No expecting the "here and now" to come but feel your physical, your soul, and the negative energy. So that *you* and only you can be responsible for the positive energy to come forth. It may be by yourself when it doesn't matter, that sure makes sense because with people you may be occupied. Though too much taking on negative energy to the point of depression is not recommended. Oh, never.

It's like he never knew how to love me, or he didn't go out of his way to. It made me out to be nothing, neither good or bad; a soul existing maybe but not exactly. Because all in all, the control he possessed depended on being good, considering the reality disappeared in how I could retaliate. The innocence was fake when he believed I wouldn't seek revenge. His words weren't working with logic in how to treat someone in order to engage in better communication. Something's wrong there, and it was not getting better. He can't expect everything to be fine with whatever he says and what sin he is in. It's like he once believed in God, but then again, we both fell into trouble. I could say I literally copied his treatment toward me, but I feel bad about it knowing how I was not able to "love" him, like it was out of my hands. Or is this the possibility of a coupledom not meant to be and I didn't know it? I was aware how "difficult" it was to lend out a helping hand. So sad on my part but it makes me blame myself, but what about him? Was he aware that this is how I felt?

I don't care whether you think that boyfriend for you is the one or he's not, just remember, "Never let him stop you for doing what your heart desires." He may be the one. But just in case he isn't, you'll find out later on because right now at this moment, you have something to take care of and that is your God-given dream and choice for your career or destiny. Refuse to let your boyfriend crush your future, even as monumental, his love means to you. If you know in your heart and mind and soul to go for a great thing, then do it.

I feel I missed out on one thing, and my ex-boyfriend would say, "Why would you need to do that?" Get off the Zoom room, whatever it may be. I felt in order for him to be "the one," I had to listen to him. What a mistake. Look what I know now.

Dangerous Me

I want to feel life, there is no reciprocation for misery.
Distorted is to achieve it through revenge because available is the
    opportunity.

I'm helpless to make a conscious decision, I'd rather not.
What's missing is empathy and in retrospect, I forsook a lot.

So far, I feel apathetic and regretful for a short-term.
My desire to be discreet, can I carry it forward and is viable to discern?

All I do is act out in times of unintentional hate.
He never intended to hurt.
Do I feel satisfied in this frame of life, where I talk back to his angry
    words?
I'm hearing responses disregarding my feelings.
I didn't listen to what he is going through.
Insulting, I get volatile, rising toward inefficacy.
Ceasing danger is to stifle me, is that true?

On My Toes

My boyfriend uses avenues to catch my attention. I conclude he is
   on my side.
Personally, I took sensitivity when he commented on general people
   and incidents that eventually provide.
He was trying to distract me from my voices. I guess walking in
   silence it's something I can't hide.

A habit to say nothing that makes sense for me to react or talk me
   "down."
It's probably better for my ego to submit all around. He just may be
   protecting the relationship to keep it sound.
I didn't see it in myself, I guess hating silence I never found.

I don't void myself of the truth. I'm myself a plain Jane. This lie could
   be a voice out of nowhere to control my self-esteem, yet the
   inclination to my impulsivity keeps me insane.
Am I oblivious to a wholesome direction comprised? Can you give an
   effort to react, brain?
Upon the empty space in my mind, to frown on my consequences,
   I refrain.

How could I right this "idea" of wrong?
My cognizance is an attitude filled with mistakes. Pretty much the
   wrong is to fuel it as make-believe. Whatever words I say is for
   my sake.
No matter how hurtful I expressed to my boyfriend, he had been oh
   so offensive.
Hey, we give and we take.

Constant Wheel

Where in the middle of my working mind can it stop and process, "Why, what is the reason?"
To say I should be better than him and I deserve better is absolute treason.
Even with my schizophrenic outbursts, can't I be worth his time and be generous with my presence every season?
Boyfriend and girlfriend seeming to bring contempt, but now I treat as appeasing.

My answer is it must be my past haunting me? For my soul hurts from mistreatment. My body included and then trashed is what I've garnered.
I can't compensate with what these bad men have done to me, a pursuit of me whatsoever never proffered.
I wonder how me and my boyfriend could be in a relationship.
I should still be grateful. It's not my boyfriend's job to deter me from what has fostered.
He loves me, regardless, and this is a story that has been authored.

My spirit lively as it is, wants to keep taking reign.
I can swallow my pride and be silent, which option is better?
To blurt nonsense, why would I want to do that, it only causes pain.
Like a conductor constantly commanding, I receive and am ready and willing.
Assigned to one place, I am not ready to switch lanes.
This part of me feels assured enough to commit unknowing.
How does this happen where it looks like I suffer mental combat, I've never been trained?

Grateful Going Forward

What would come of this relationship, how would I know to stay
    with my boyfriend?
Is he who I would keep if my world came to an end?
When I met him, the decision based on all occurrence.
The matter had been important he's in my heart, I can't let him go
    again.
My world had been a transition to go through another psychotic
    breakdown, I couldn't do it on my own.
This time, damaging personalities trying to relate and grab at a
    chance.
But my boyfriend had been the suitable bachelor making me feel
    grown.
I always longed for the unfamiliar, yet with my friends, I had not
    been guided wrong.
Their tastes for the classy girls, my gratitude pops up and wonder-
    ment stays strong.
Working out life together is a dancing step of back and forth.
Through symbiosis, it helps me. I help him between us; it's what love
    to store.
Almost as if other people don't matter but who's to say?
We care about them and each other every single day.

Handling All of It

I hear delusions and on top of that, adding this reality of getting
    them to be "something" to make myself at ease?
It's a distorted world to think that I can erase it.
When I just want to let it go from my mind at least.

Heart-wrenching to come to a point and see if I will control myself
    or combust to the point of no return.
I had an issue with self-sabotage. I disagree and disobey the angelic,
    caring voice no matter how stern.

What's better than living in an environment where the schizophrenia
    is a slight episode.
When I walk into a psychiatric office, and my overall problem was
    shyness, it won't dictate my mode.

I'm all in for the help, for one reason and one reason only.
This time of relaxation is like meditation and having someone in
    front of me listen.
All the while recognizing always that my mind is a place, I'd like to
    be homely.

In public, all I had to do was be discreet, avoid mistakes.
When I am the victim to be, I open my mouth. There's the sign, now
    their target is locked.
All because I couldn't decipher beyond the shadow of a doubt, the
    "kindness included" was fake.

Trying to Love

Normally, what I hear I expel a sort of mixed understanding and tend
to hold him accountable for insulting.
My driven outbursts, I gave no thought in being further volatile. I
can't brush off these as nothing.

My boyfriend is important to me. What he says I take to heart.
In reciprocation, I want to give off light, not misery, and so I do my
part.

Opportunity to achieve is available in form of revenge sadly, to relieve
my helplessness.
In an episode, running from a conscious decision I would rather not.
For my boyfriend shows selflessness.

What's missing from my bottle of emotions is empathy.
I am short-term apathetic but placing regret all on him is heresy.
My desire to be discreet: is it viable with these times of unintentional
hate?
He must be hurt when my frame is satiated by talking back feeling
so irate.

Isn't it about what he's going through and his feelings?
I was sitting pretty, hearing disregard to mine, yet I never listened
to what he meant and what he's going through because I had a
moment of personal solitude. I felt he was stealing.

Once Again, I Must Face

Are my former experiences with men blindly lived out as being taken
    advantage of?
I take my healing as a way to lash out at my boyfriend.
Is this what it has become push to shove?

It was cruel and unnecessary, and our blessed relationship, it felt all
    I did was blame
These past men took a semblance of a life full of hope never staying,
    leaving shame.

Being used made me having satisfaction with happiness within the
    confines of marriage nonexistent.
My depressive state has become below average, the disappointment
    easily consistent.

Conniving men shouldn't be called men.
When they make enjoyment of life and bliss end.

Is real happiness with normal factorings too much to handle?
The extremity of getting high off of control and power, will it blow
    out the candle?

Being glad with what I have, my childlike heart appears.
I know why because with functioning first and foremost my erratic
    behavior jumps out of the way and the demons start to veer.

Settled

Am I convinced with his comment that I need to make a change?
I realize this is what he is saying.
How about I believe he's not confirming "this is what it has come
   to?"
No, it's just a basic regard to, "Like how that happened. Well, that's
   just the way it is."
Men are simple, and he's probably assuring me things happen, "Oh
   well."

Was he trying to attack me? Oh, not at all.
More like an epiphany to come to this, even though it sure seems I'm
   needing to get used to it.
"To get used to it" is more like an excuse.
I've seen myself react to each comment of his.
Memory of taking it lighthearted is doubtful.

Living every moment of every day with me accepting the presence of
   miniscule inklings.
The event where a thing falls out of place.
He expresses himself in the way he can to affect what could be a
   casual mood.
Happy is the way to go and to be thankful of this, yes, I should.

No Backing Down

Whenever I try out a sentiment to change him, is he calling me weird
or the action?
It never works out.
Preparing for an argument, I may though I never try to believe he is
normal with normal thoughts.
His views seem idiosyncrasies unbeknownst to him, looking like
mania.
Does he know what's going on to presume at least his behavior?
I decipher my ideas of his source of etiquette all the while my schizo-
phrenia speaks over him.

I am now involving myself in this bantering, going along with run-
ning notions.
He says he's not in control with what I say.
Ever think it could be more than my disease?
Is it having another diagnosis added to this belief?
Are we now discussing my volatile mood swings where I flip one
hundred eighty degrees?
Are these the days where it's more than a fight?
Time to conquer the tragedy of truth in labor toward my rescue.
I must get over it for I can't argue.

Are You the One?

"Good times and laughter do not make a lasting foundation," an
actual quote.
A necessity factor apart from "accessory" cookie cutter model perfect
relationship.
Kind of like a thirty-year-old marriage can end up in divorce.
Having a past lover being totally in love, yet it didn't work out.
In good spirits, no one wins except to extract all one can get with
who is not the one.
My boyfriend, not the bad guy as I conceal, not analyzing his com-
mitment struggles.
Am I the only one stuck in this bubble?
Attempting to recognize beyond my emotions what I really have
been needing.

I am not a stagnant partner, only reluctantly staying.
I confer the days are natural beckoning to overcome, by firmly being
devoted
I am assured it's not a game I'm playing.
I know when someone needs care like I do.
And I am his share.

Human

Through a veil shielding you from my heart,
I view you distorted held by superficiality and I accept.
In my own world surrounded by what I can do,
I get surprised by you being human.

It seemed so simple to present myself.
I've been caught up in my arrogance giving no effort in uncondi-
    tional love.
I observe yet keep going on to live the life.
Striving with your part, me shrinking in mine.
I look selfish when it comes to authenticity given.

At one point, I sought solace, the other a clue into what made us be.
I must've relaxed my hold on tense grips.
I couldn't let go of the mundane outlooks staying the same.
Yet my eyes opened to forgiveness.
It was all that was left.
I don't know what else to do.
All I wanted was to have and never realized I had you.

Holding Me

If again our relationship rocks unexpectedly, I will solve figuring he
    is the one.
Whether I admit it or wonder, the night I lay next to him, I won't be
    able to sleep.
While a second person's voice cries in my head, and he'll turn from
    his side to me.

I am held now, and my restless soul starts to dimmer.
My mind softens in nature and in topic.
I stay with him, but I deserve no credit.
My words have become of no worth when it's out of my control, and
    he's no care to hurt.

By day, a satisfied ego is of no benefit.
His pain is expressed of seeing me do a 180-degree flip in personality.
His ideas of who I am I decipher as an attack and as true as they may be
I regard the delusion he's denying my existence, along with his tone,
    it's all so real to me.
What can I do but fight the demon from not taking over?

To Give In

He responds to my craziness.
The only reason being for it to happen is if it made me act on it.
I guess someone's got to give in.
In all retrospect, it's what stirred me to move.
To apologize in what has happened for a reason.
Along with compromise, I agreed from the background of connec-
    tion we have.
This is what made me choose.

Hearing can be a sign but to take everything in likeness is not an
    ideology to rely in.
Almost convincing me to answer my psychosis.
Faith would be based upon truth.
When you "heard the truth."
Wouldn't there be a chance not to repeat a mistake, once learning to
    pick up what works?
What's sane, so I check the spirits, telling me whether I can pursue
    this way or not.

Second to None

Every time you apply love, I want to see the action.
You speak, you verbalize sometimes out of the blue.
I haven't experience such before, I don't know how to get satisfaction.
It is at these times, I try to retaliate in order to communicate it's true.

Who you are compared to me, you are so active?
So many thoughts of you make it seem I'm done.
Criticisms from you I take to heart, I feel like I've had it.
What you did to me, I wanted to get even, but that's no fun.

There were moments I couldn't believe this was me.
My anger, my attitude, where was this all coming from?
Can I give in and wonder no more? It's crazy.
Escaping too valid, schizophrenia revealed in me second to none.

Shelter Me Sane

How do I handle my decisions when I cannot even process my
feelings?
I was at a place, my conscience I couldn't detect.
When I see who my friends are and not these monsters chasing me,
only then can there be stability.
But first of all, a house to stay in, no more roaming alone would
make me feel at ease.
Especially dialing the right phone number because I remember and
not the wrong number for when desperate.
Sad for times like these, the memory of going to church steadily has
become the past.
No longer seeing the culmination of a reputation ever to last.
My lifestyle not only seems different, it actually is.
On top of that is change to go through, for the street can be reckless.
I cannot handle it.
Thank goodness for those along the way.
Like angels helping me go from night to day.
Not knowing where else to go, they helped me stay under control.
The streets are not a place for me.
Help me, God, to understand what it means to be happy.
Is it this withdrawal of thoughts that is preventing me of a memory
happy?
Expounding the hardship of this fact slowly escapes my joyfulness
once here.
Going away from my head, or it never appeared.
Whatever happened to being immersed with racing thoughts?
Experiencing apathy in thoughtless silence.

In these remaining moments, I choose to be gleeful.
Can't I at least exhibit positive, outgoing mumblings?
Murmurs or small statements, I know it's not much altogether.
Or even attractive, I believe.

Boyfriend, before you doze off for the night, I want you to grasp I'm
    doing my best.
All you do is worry about me, don't you?
It's an ongoing test with me and you, yet 24-7, it feels like we're
    blessed.

From this point, without you, there's nothing else I could do.
You had to have belonged in my life one way or another.
So much growing and becoming to.
I have never cared much without it being available.
Do you see it's not your fault, my lover?

There All Along

Taking in time that has passed
Is it because where I am at I don't see?
Are my dreams of absolutes daunting?
Measures of apathy are wasted trying to fix them.
How can I understand their destination?
Lack of words come about with no understanding.
Is this the life of knowledge in reality?
All day in my head are burdens of being burdened
Going toward the light couldn't have been anything, could it?
Each day, I linger on a premise.
Will my routine change or my attitude differ?
Do I have important thoughts on it whatsoever?
With fine opportunities leading to promotion
I finally want peace of mind.
Amidst realization, I wake up in broad daylight.
In my moment of personalization, I shone bright.
A few seconds of gratitude I obtained.
That's when I stepped into truth.
My love went on silently supposedly
I went searching for what's happening.
Little did I know, I had a relationship to work on and still do.

Criminal

When a mentally ill is guilty of a crime, do they mean it?
Or because a crime is committed, the criminal receives punishment.
Yes, it happens. Punishment for what it's worth.

Such is love based on evidence and judgment or intent of defendant.
I feel like a lawyer having a client to represent
My job, my life, no longer independent.
How can the honor go without evidence, incriminating with self-ful-
    filling bias?
Is a corrupt judge signifying liaison to other criminals?
Question: is he friends of the normal appearance to society, the true
    criminals yet on the down low?
Particularly partial, a defining factor to find those ready to convict
    the innocent being they are mentally ill.
By the way, it's *not needed* to be falsely accused of crimes.
It is not a crime to love even though I am crazy.

Withdrawing Refined

It is to no avail when I want my boyfriend to solve the problem, I
    get angry.
You can guess why.
He makes me think, and he talks back. I'm trying to dwell on my
    emoting to get by.

I feel secluded trying to hide the fact my schizophrenia is effective.
My chance is to withdraw, but his no response drives me crazy.
I'm different. I think less normally when it comes to arguments.

Am I attacked because I need to be alone, or am I compelled to
    entertain?
My mind had already left and withheld its peace.
Like a broken record player needing to cease
I leave no pleasantry, no melody, no anything.

Nasty fights, wishing he'd stop talking.
To get a clue, I don't do this for sport.
Resulting is a twisted form of communication where he thinks I
    enjoy.

With Understanding

With boundaries do I need to rebound
At the same time do I look at who I express it to.
An understanding, it can be reached I don't know how. I would snap.
The other persons explanation is completely void; I pass judgment.
Is it imaginary or real? This reasoning must be meaning I'm sorry.
They can't be right; I have a disorder called schizophrenia.
I blow up when confronted needlessly, subliminally.
I had gone schizo since I was diagnosed.
Or either I'm seen and known as schizo, so I'm just being me.
I don't know.
There is no need to go over that some intuitions run deep.
I can please people and be hospitable.
An unexpected symptom or an unlikely dispute.
I definitely need space even if the concerned is in the room.
The solutions for me is I'd rather, like the other person, forget the
    whole episode and move on.
Maybe unusual but what can you expect from me?
My mind runs fast. A lesson I refuse on how I responded. I refuse to
    be berated further because I know what I did.
It's hard to tell whether I'm regarding my place for snapping.
I can't promise it won't happen again. What it is, how should I say
    it—I see myself "revealed without compromise or caring on
    intent."
For it not to happen again, I know is uncertain.
Do I have good intent, oh, like you wouldn't believe?

Mood

Always needing to be in good spirits and no interruptions.
Blaming my boyfriend on my change of mood or thought, so
    dangerous.

The scene is he denies what he hasn't felt in heart.
I'm opportunistic when it comes to his behavior.
If he told me he was interested in watching a movie, he now denies it.
Am I blowing up for an extra input I apparently had dropped?

Nothing I would say mattered by saying something related to nor-
    mal, I presume to my peers.
Another reminder of my diagnosis.
I sink deeper into shutting off any form of communication.
Or is it had I even started?

What Else

Are these my symptoms being used in a way to procure straight to
the impulse?
How about the delusions?
Is it only I am acting on it?
I couldn't stop and realize it was a mistake.
Convicted, he needed to suffer for making me suffer.

I respond with whatever bad mood.
On the top of my head to more like tip of the tongue.
I'd better maintain mental stability than my looks.
His request will now be based on the fact he doesn't know what to
expect.
While I am treated unkindly in an unlikely way.
Either held by an unconscious grudge or my lack of understanding
to the atmosphere.
As if I'm never considering the man's needs.

Intent

I can't seem to accept he won't change. It's not every minute I think of my misery now.

But it's when his lack of normalcy gets expressed when we fight, I get frustrated.

I'm not trying to change him; I need more of a conscience telling me to back off.

It's a pursuit of bashing words.

I see my pride win over, and I sense hearing that his will get worse, my "self-proclaimed injustice inflicted over me."

I ride out the defense I had no idea it was even me.

I almost think, "Did I rehearse this?"

Because the meanness flows so easily out.

Vengeful action could be rarely but surely carried out, especially when given the "must be" a form of knowing punishment on intended boyfriend.

Sad thing is I feel maybe my responsibility was to let go, but why I choose the wrong letting go?

I was getting rogue be it toward him.

I was in seriousness to forgive to let go.

How am I to delude vicious intent by somehow saying the worst is the best way?

Since it is a way at least. To make some progress, to feel releasing of hurt.

Though every intent to be good came with positive thoughts, I still had frustrated hateful thoughts.

If in passing unchecked, all to do I try it out.

Yet even when I'm good right then appears an onset. It surprises I believe.

It is that I need to work out a deeper hurt or trauma that's not so much regarding my boyfriend.

With Him

Just got to admit, this is the man I must deal with, and all men will
    have imperfections.
Not saying in the realm to move on but so that our relationship can
    grow.
Let murmurs happen from side glances when we're in public, what-
    ever my regarding my coupling with him.

It doesn't have to be about him, but when it does have to be, I take
    the duty to *love* fully.
Not everything is about him at these certain times when I think of him.

If he cannot handle his pride, he is not narcissistic.
Every man needs to feel like he is a man owning his manhood.

Exposed

Say to hold a box is to have a normal capability.

Like the inside of a box can hold love; it is when on the outside, there
   is the difference.

The mentally ill have love only lying on the outside, where it easily
   burns off the from the simile of sun's rays or outside symptoms.

Love is like that box, having it be freely received and emptied, but my
   craziness has love staying on the surface.

Difficult to determine if it is felt.

Can I visually or tangibly sense it is not hating?

I'm not understood as deeply or long enough as others, or is it the
   other way around?

I'm still part of the box I call love.

I treat each problem with space and patience with him in this matter.

For he may have ideas I'm not reaching him like others or in how it
   could be.

Diagnosis

This imagination of something is so lifelike.
Your character of someone, of that to be someone else none other than.
And then, being able to see reality as a contrast because it's so lifelike enmeshed, almost subtle.
But the tolerance hurts in coupledom. I want my partner to be consistent.
For example, a lack of explanation can provide irrational fear.
In the case of my boyfriend, does he have an "achievement accordingly" obsession, rather than manic or depressive phases?
Needing things done in organized manner in this way deems suitable as obtained in his mind.

How many months have I felt it would get better?
I believed with a numbness and then only to believe.
And then it was an in-love situation,
At the same time stagnant.
The feeling came inching in on how it was like the initial suffering…
To be continued, yet the end.

Not Everything Though

My steps seem to lead me.
As a path was already beneath me.
It's not that I reach out.
But with every turn, I'm mesmerized with tolerance and silent correction
Even urging how I could leave yet finally stems a need to stay.

It's the likelihood of being blindsided.
Then I see his point of view, it's provided.
To me to be only plain to see.
I must tell myself that I do cause trouble.
What he does is vital and only to better.
Good thing I recognize I have not become nothing in anyone's eyes.

Every day a steady awakening or a chance to praise.
Not all the time searching for the bright side and that's the priority.
Just to keep moving on with life like we were meant to be.
I am his helper and not his sole everything.
I am for him when I can; somehow, I believe in him.

Accepting Forgiveness

The scent of flowers at once in hand.
The sense of glee in this particular man.
Never in attracting to me and linking
This an apathetic view on mania and love.

Resignation is the atrocious words, then the next minute so
    precocious.
Pertinent to no target, no end goal am I to be jealous.

Have I stood right in his eyes?
Is he taking me for a demon?
He really does love me I realize.
For the unspoken sadness birthed to life.

If apologies were well-received, would you accept even with my dry
    tears?
Not one has dropped only to disappear.
Remorse to appear, oh but to at least bow my head.

I wanted love for love's sake.
Even promising myself to be that great.
Yet we belong exactly where we're at.
Obliging to no one, he didn't want to let me go.

Return

Your identity, Danny.
Do you think I'm unaware?
Of the dangers of rebellion,
The chase of the unknown you dare?
What would happen to those you love?
When they hear of your choice.
To ease your life into oblivion,
Because you couldn't handle the voice.
The only voice that tells the truth.
Is the One who's always been with you.
He wanted you as His child.
He sacrificed to be alive so life would ensue.
If it weren't for our Lord.
And what He thinks of His children,
The history destined could be forgotten.
He was always nearby. Looking out.
Faith starts when you hear.
Danny, if you only understand what God is saying,
That you are His precious child of God, worth it all.
Then maybe running back to Him is not bad.
It may take months; it may take years.
Maybe till the end.
All I want is for you to trust Him anyway; God steers.

Voiding Choices

Once I was the blue diamond in the treasure chest.
To hold and to cherish.
You left me alone, my sparkles, my shine glaring.

Going on through the motions.
While in secret, the emotions blazing a path of resentment.
Nor could I reach anyone with the truth about my struggle in resist-
     ing the confusion bared.

It's getting better or so it seems, that's what I observe.
This time, I'm smarter or more is it that I'm more susceptible.
I entertain subconsciously my way to deeper awakening.

Is there something I'm made clear of evidentially on signs pointing
     dear?
How is this happening?
How can I walk away from someone who follows me but doesn't
     pursue any solution?

Maybe Now

Has it been that long?
No, not nearly an hour.
A coldhearted battle to figure out what?
To let me know I'm schizophrenic?
That I'm the one that does the same things over and over again?
Do I speak in haste or respond in hate?
That I need to be treated that way.

One thing, if I never listen, neither do you.
I'd take from example, but you present yourself king?
Do you believe that's healthy to do for the rest of your life?

Then I realize, what have I done?
What did I do to deserve that though?
So I am now reconsidering going back.
I won't though. Perhaps, it wasn't that.

Relax

Resting on earth, leaning on strength.
Reality is, it's no walk in the park.
It's like, no matter how I try my best, I'm left in the dark.

Heaven had once been our dwelling.
Up there, we were all one and the same.
Being born, there had been no telling,
Of humble beginnings or a lifetime of strain.

Some are allotted this life or that.
Either in poverty can be a spark of hope.
At a dinner table can be plenty of wine and fat.
Without peace, its hanging on the end of a rope.

High-Class/Low-Class

Fame has gotten some fans and those hidden.
Secretly awaiting gain for their own.
Not every success is free for winning.
Money is paid back, given, and loaned.

The relationships are but futile.
In closed caption, theirs is wholeness for oneself.
It's not a bad thing to reconcile.
As long as those friends bless your health.

The losses are taken when once a bit of honor turned to tragedy.
To conceive the reality of a turnaround in life.
When once before it was all worth worrying about.
The degradation seems only understood by you.

I look back at my actions,
Tell me what I've done.
Call me out on that behavior.
It was crazy, yes.

To be a schizophrenic, I can't let go.
It's what I'll always hold on to.
Every day, every hour.
But to make a mistake, is not because I hold a title less likely for
    better moods.

I've done wrong to be corrected, to have it pointed out and made
    aware.
I shan't hear twice on being a schizophrenic.
It's like calling me a fool, so "look at your stupid mess!"

I've been wrong before, allow me a chance to explain.

Mind doesn't give up things easily of trigger words.
Triggering because it hurts.
If I could choose it not to make me react, I would.
But this life has made known such things are not irreversible.
Or now you know, we will perhaps never mount up to what we could
    be.

Let Me Say

There are these times I remember,
And then it comes back how it started.
The beginning of me publicly announcing my frustration, barely
love a consideration.

I am a bit hurt within myself,
And taken aback of my audacity.
I realize audacity but my careless apathy toward selfishness.

I saw myself above you and even me.
I had this deserving attitude to arrogantly have you serve the goddess
in need of praise.

That was not correct at all.
I'd be hiding such pride and made it like I was appalled and that had
to make sense.

Forgive me, Danny, for you know how to treat me.
Not everybody else has been the greatest.
You have been the love who knew me.
Who knew that I struggled but pretended it didn't matter until it did?

I thank you for that.

Unkept

I have this limitation.
As if I have undergone a regimen.
Seems I have let down my reins.

Once so ladylike, there goes irritation.
Now, the volcano gurgled again.
Keeping sanity is in vain.

Setting boundaries is that unlike me.
I just wanted to be accepted.
Do the same since it's necessary to be done.

Feeling equality is one thing.
Being different to just be is the struggle.
Having a flow to maintain has disappeared.

The once stability had I taken for granted.
Wanting peace was a wish almost dismissing glory.
What was I thinking, having both at my fingertips?

Stronger

Before I met you, I thought of someone else.

Somehow who had been with me I considered that guy able to take me in, but he never did.

I tend to fall for those kinds of "guys." What if that guy was you and I made a mistake?

Or is it because I wondered as such was when I made the biggest mistake.

If the truth was further, I couldn't find it.

Maybe if I stayed in the relationship with you, it must mean we were meant to be.

That's what I did because I saw no other way out.

Wait out the storm for a whirlwind it was.

Every day, I try to get it and figure out the reason. Is it me?

Do I not know how to make choices?

Can I acknowledge the red flags or continue with understanding and letting things go?

Do I believe it's all better?

Am I struggling, or am I the struggle to you? So we're both even. If I can't remember when you last loved me, is that wrong?

I compare our love to waking up, not remembering how I love you.

I feel lacking in how to express true affectionate desire. Isn't it me now? I can't be with anyone else.

You put up with me like I have put up with you. Of course, love between two isn't perfect.

At times, it was hard to come out and complain. And I have to admit, I could've let out more with any little I did get to.

My heart feels so constricted like it's all in or escape, no other choice.

Yet I hear a voice tell me you love me.

All I do is anticipate your irrational decisions. Then time goes on, and I see you do things out of love.

Today, it brightened my eyes, and my heart that you do give effort.
You are not a bad person, no, you just have too much to say.
And you've been through a lot.
That makes you strong. I hope you get stronger with me.

Into Reality

As we talk about the public scene, I describe myself being embar-
    rassed afterward and not during.
I see you as a target, and I spew to break down what I see needs
    diminishing.
Can I stop finally, I can only try?
You know that I have a disease, that I have angry outbursts.
I must know that too.
I commend you for loving me.
You stick by me you do.
All this time, when I wreak havoc, you managed to talk me into
    reality.
It's like you never stopped loving me.
I have a special man.
Thankful, yes. Keep me in bliss. I am happy.

Wasn't happiness where I had to be?
Am I calculating the complications of my relationship unnecessarily?
I go down with the ship, deluding myself.
I keep ignoring the benefits of my day, and what it beholds.
It's going to be a final decision. My day is filled with opportunities so
    therefore, blessed to go forward.
Stepping into reality.

More than Enough

When can I stop my determination?
This high, this energy that deems only negativity?
He hurts and I only get apathetic. Two days ago, I imagined I could
    love him.
A spark of feeling, this is what I desired.

Now, things collapsing, falling apart.
A new day and I feel awaken to frustration. Is it my past mistakes
    coming to haunt me?
I am only a sick girl. I blame not the trauma.
But shouldn't I see the truth instead?

Maybe I went through more than enough.
To comprehend healing is what I was pursuing. I fend off believing
    I'm wrong.
Yet is this correct, to be blind from the bigger picture?

Once I grab hold of an excuse, I blame you.
No way could it be my fault.
I have no flaws. Surely none that I own. Then I conclude reality, I, a
    firecracker, fierce with my fist once or twice before.
I see him sad more than I. I can't cry much no, rather I brag.
Communicating is better for me than my partner.
That can be a lie, for my attempts are worse when crazy.

What Now?

I look down at my feet. Or I look out because I'm sitting.
Legs rested on the bed; I'm thinking.
Back to the wall, with this room set up, it's fitting.

Now, there is a decision internal. To protect my heart is eternal.
I agree to keep myself from the ache.
But it's a fight to choose what I underestimate. Yes, I talk of my ways,
    how I am not capable.
My relationship show how far I've come, now that's palpable.

I succumb to any recommendation for my temper is running out.
Intimidating it is, he'll test the result and say "Face it!" I want to
    shout!
The love is immense but just a feeling.
The situation doesn't make sense. Whether I get better, the thought
    turns my head reeling.
It's the truth of his love that's present. The reality of schizophrenia
    has the suggestion be negligent.
It is to keep my destiny in the will of God.
Rescued by a medical drug. Do not be ashamed. It's hard but healthy
    just the same.

Pleasing People

Reflect on things past.
Well, I tried to please people without rationality.
Is there a reward for that? How long will today last?
The items, the circumstances still there, but it did produce some
    effect or change.
And it was to show myself stand out.
I'm not pretentious, I have a kind stare.

How do I succumb to the success of that memory?
What counts when I must leave that barrenness behind?
What is done is needed as pleasing and is emotionally painstaking.
Not as easy anymore in graduality.

Accommodate the action and the duty.
No matter how meticulous it once was,
Is now simple if I but breathe in.
To remember the needs, I need to attain to.
To know when love takes me is where I am truly.

Round and Round

Doesn't he recognize delight?
Even when it arrives, he seems unsatiated.
Grieving is he due and taking time?
Mourning properly or pushing it away?
Self-awareness toward identity should shun negative affirmations.

We don't accept our relationship as easily as others.
Are we doing our best indefinitely?
I could've chosen less to punish him.
I need not alleviate my pain by him and him only.

Never nullified how I feel, although numbing at times.
Since the last I repented to be mean.
I turned out fine but for that moment of triumph.
Later, it was outlandish for it rose again.

Despondent

Every day is intertwined with my breathing.
To live with the waking up to life seeking.
How do I tell I get mesmerized by your avenues to pursue our love?
Filling it with memories of togetherness to get by and what prosper-
    ity may come of.
We get comfortable sometimes, and the expectations rise.
Excuse my disregard, I can't speak. Please see it in my eyes.
My aloofness, my spacing couldn't have stemmed from my heart.
I have a mind that wants to escape and forget how it starts.

Getting to Love

I assumed I had it.
But assuming can't help what's needed.
Did I see the effort was worthless, at least my attention had been
heeded?
I can't figure out or get past what is the answer.
I seem to dwell on the demon, not the latter.
Will I come out worse than before, or do I falter to beginning over?
Starting out where I was, I continue.
I never see my demon as a realization.
It's more an outburst, I don't want to call my own.
The only important thing is love, I want to hold.
Ironically, the expression leads toward selfishness so bold.
Love is patient, love is kind. It does not envy, it does not boast, it is
not proud.
It is not rude, it is not self-seeking, it is not easily angered, it keeps
no record of wrongs.
Love does not delight in evil but rejoices in the truth. It always pro-
tects, always trusts, always hopes, always perseveres.
Love never fails.

Bit of Peace

Such days harbored by my paranoia and hallucinating voices.
I crave any sort of ease unconsciously.
At a time of peace do I comprehend a bit of frustration.
Not because of the comparison to quietness and the future voices.
No, because now I am more aware of what I need to do in the present
and the life I behold had been schizophrenia and will be.
Thankful for the presence of my boyfriend who made the troubles
disappear.
They went without my knowledge, and I feel the gradual lull deep
inside that wants fulfillment.
Crying out in question and appalled by the passing differentiation
of two worlds.
Unbeknownst to me, I start getting frantic much easier to correct my
boyfriend.
If I were by myself, I have nothing like him in the duration of my days.

Less symptoms of voices and hallucinations. Maybe.
Much more distraction and a supernatural mind? Yes.
Is it vice versa? Pretty much so. As long as this, the symptoms are
getting better.

About the Author

Jeannie Choi was born in Astoria, New York, to South Korean immigrants. Raised in Great Neck, Long Island, New York, and Maui, Hawaii, she found her passion for arts, such as sketching, writing, drama, and modeling. As of recent, Jeannie has been quite accomplished in her watercolor paintings and her newest endeavor, her first literary work as a published author.

She has a younger brother who enjoys church activities and has a seminary degree. Religion and faith in a higher power are what she sets her mind to so she can succeed. At age seven, Jeannie started windsurfing with her family; taught by her dad. He then decided to move the family to the Hawaiian Islands. By that time, Jeannie was thirteen. She now resides in the Washington state.

CPSIA information can be obtained
at www.ICGtesting.com
Printed in the USA
BVHW030759031122
650634BV00009B/179

9 781638 609254